The

ANUNNAKI THEOREM

A CONCISE PERSPECTIVE ON HUMANITY'S ORIGINS IN REGARD TO THE DIVINE …

[2022 Reissue]

The Anunnaki Theorem

Eduardo Fidencio Cano

Contact@esotericeddie.com

INTRODUCTION

Thank you for taking an interest in this knowledge. May this visit into my work be an interesting and useful stop on your personal journey to wherever it is you want to go. I would like the reader to know that in no way is this work meant to be extensive but rather a confronting and momentary expansion on the subject matter at hand. This is a reissue of my first book, which was poorly edited. I apologize to anyone who bought the original and attempted to sit through the poorly written work. It's no excuse, but I was much younger when I initially published the book and was too enthusiastic about what I had to say. I have heavily edited the original, omitting a lot of what I felt was unnecessary, adding much more useful information. I hope you enjoy it!

Table of Contents

Chapter 1

Divinity

In this day and age where nuclear war is more bound to happen than ever, where protest against governments is raging and rampant, where destruction of our environment is caused by our greed, where our hatred has separated us, where science is replacing the love for universal spiritually, where no messiah is to be found, where no clear voice of God is spoken strong enough to even shake the frowns on a fraction of the earth, one might ask themselves if God is even real. I've asked myself that question plenty of times with a conditioned urge to battle my doubt. I was born Catholic and raised Christian. I was brought up intensely believing the Devil was a real entity that was out to destroy me and perform the most gruesome things to me in Hell if I did not confess Jesus to be my savior, obey the Church authorities or my elders. I was also taught and even warned by my own peers not to question the Bible, that it was the worst of all sins! This hostility confounded me throughout my childhood. What was this strict indoctrination all about? I felt that there was something more to this mundane life, but I just didn't feel like I would ever get close to that with the institutions of the world in the way. They box us into safe and predictable mind states, ones that won't question the status quo.

Throughout my life I've had instances that revealed bits of hidden knowledge and through these incremental steps toward higher learning I was left wanting to know more. That quest led me down intriguing paths of self-education but also into dark and mysterious, sometimes unfathomable experiences. Our minds can break as we shatter and shift paradigms; leaving all we thought was true as lies, we enter a new state of profoundness. As I grew, I noticed the obvious hypocritical preaching of man, the strange and obscure teachings of sacred texts that very few ever questioned, and the fear that everyone had about doubting authority, whether it be spiritual or legal. I was rebellious at a young age and questioned everything. I was led to knowledge by way of sheer chance or divine will but mostly because of my diligence in seeking knowledge. Constant analysis of my surroundings gave me insight and wisdom. Constant reflecting on my inner struggles and psychological complexes gave me insight and wisdom as to how a mind works in coherence with a soul and body. It's important to self-reflect especially when learning new information that goes against what you've been taught. We must check in with ourselves and take a pace that will allow the massive realizations to take hold without completely eradicating our minds. As the old sayings go, seek and ye shall find but be careful what you wish for. I did just that and I guess because of it my learning of the truth that I am going to share here officially began around 2006. For me it was the summer going into seventh grade. I had been listening to radical hip-hop music about consciousness, illuminati, aliens and all sorts of mind-opening things. I was habitually smoking reefer and thinking deeply. It was then that my mind was opened. It happened in my cousin's room; he too was on this journey with me at just one year younger than I. Staring at a one-dollar bill and the strange seals on the back I pondered and did so for a while as my cousin and I

conversed about esoteric subjects. Right then and there,

as I was sitting in his computer chair, we decided to look

up the meanings of those seals. If the Internet is more

than just a digital communications apparatus then it

certainly is somewhat of a portal. What I opened in my

mind from that day on was a never-ending surge of

knowledge that my soul had been asking for since I was

born, ever since my first encounter with the enigmatic

world of the Church and its strange paintings and statues.

Upon researching the history of the cryptic symbols on

the back of our everyday currency, I stumbled into a

world of Freemasonry. I found that in the early half of

the 1900s, Henry A. Wallace, later vice president, had

President Franklin D. Roosevelt officially approve the

sigils to be used for our great seal. Wallace and Roosevelt were both members of the Freemason organization. Now, I assume the reader is aware of the basics of this group and what they've been accused of doing. On the front they are a fraternal order with legendary roots going all the way to biblical times. They have a doctrinal structure like that of the Boy Scouts wherein you earn degrees and are bestowed with more knowledge as you move up the ranks. Their entire fraternity is philosophically centered around the symbolism and mythology of the ancient mysteries surrounding the Bible and other ancient tales. The degrees are also represented by the symbols, tools and practices of a medieval mason like that of a compass and level. They claim that through their rituals and ceremonies, an unpolished person is carefully crafted, like a stone into a polished marble, from an apprentice into a perfected moral character. This order has been behind the building of many magnificent sacred lodges around the world where they hold their secret meetings. More exciting than that they claim to be the direct descendants of the infamous Knights Templar of the thirteenth century. The Templar were the first Christian army, fighting for the Church, but eventually they came across some piece of knowledge that changed their attitude. Not only growing in structure and power, eventually having enough influence and economy to rival the Church, the Templar seemingly started to practice some occult beliefs, mystical forms of Christianity at the very least. Mostly because of their influence, but also because of their rogue beliefs, the Templar were condemned and taken down by the Church with their leader Jacque DeMolay being burned at the stake in the early years of the 1300s. Just like the Templar it is said that the Freemasons of today hold ancient artifacts or knowledge lost to the rest of humanity, which has become the central role of their purpose. They are the preservers of ancient wisdom or so they say. Because of their mysterious attributes it has been claimed by many scholars and authors that they've had nefarious agendas, all guiding the world into a specific system that the Freemasons will eventually hold control over. Whether or not that is true what is apparent is their reverence for what they call the "Eye of Providence." It's exactly what we would find on the back of our US one-dollar bill; it's an all-seeing eye with sunrays protruding around it. The symbol has been used many times over in Masonic art and insignia. For the Masons this eye is the symbol of the Creator or "Providence," who is overseeing all things.

And chaotic as it may seem, life is being carefully crafted toward a righteous means by this careful inspection and crafting of the Eye of Providence. The single eye being used as a symbol of divinity has been widely used throughout the world for various reasons. In sixteenth-century Christian art, the eye was used as a symbol for God as well, as can be seen in Pontormo's 1525 *Supper at Emmaus*. Of course, the more famous would be the Egyptian Eye of Horus, which can be seen as a symbol of protection, God or even the "third eye." This symbol of the eye and divinity is far spread and usually has a similar connotation. To the Freemasons, divinity is expressed in the structural order of nature. The eye is sometimes replaced with a *G*, which could mean God but could also be interpreted as geometry. The Freemasons also refer to their God as the "Great Architect." In their worldview, everything works cohesively in a system of duality. This is

further explained by famous nineteenth-century

Freemason philosopher Albert Pike. In his astounding

authoritative book *Morals and Dogma*, he explains this to

some degree saying:

"This doctrine of the Genii, depositaries of the Universal

Providence, was intimately connected with the Ancient Mysteries,

and adopted in the sacrifices and initiations … The Gods charge

them to assist, and to distribute punishment and blessing … thus

the Genii or angels differed in character like men, some being good

and some evil …"

To the occultist it is understood that there is a balance in

the universe between forces of light and dark. Divinity to

the occultist such as Pike is the understanding of this

system, harnessing it within oneself, knowing that all is

just. The Great Architect has administered the forces of

good and evil to bring about this justice. So, in this realization they trust its eye, its judgment. Along with this, within Masonic lodges there is the symbol of the checkered floor with the black-and-white tiles. This is another symbol of the structured universe where the forces of light and dark are neatly placed accordingly to their purpose.

Before the official dawning of the obverse seal in the 1930s by Roosevelt's administration, the seal had gone through variations, going all the way back to America's founding. Each variation had some aspect of the "eye" in it and was produced with Masonic iconography, such as the 1782 version worked up by the Third Great Seal Committee, which presented William Barton's basic thirteen-step pyramid with an eye on top. The now Latin mottoes that cast over the pyramid and eye roughly translate as "Favor Our Undertaking." This was taken from the *Aeneid*, an epic written by the Roman poet Virgil. It was from a passage where a prayer was said to the god Jupiter, in hopes for a victorious success. It was dictated by the son of the protagonist Aeneas, right before he slew his enemy. Although obscure, through these symbols it is clearly stated by our Founding Fathers, that we are a nation under God and in this God we shall trust. In these revelations about the meaning and reasoning behind our great seal it should be understood that the pious veracity of our nation isn't all based on a Christian background but under the broad array of the human perception of God. The Freemasons, with their occult-like ambiguity, believe in a divine Creator and hold themselves accountable to it. Just what god that is, is up for interpretation.

Every person has their own personal god. The many names and archetypes we've concocted to portray the concept of an ultimate God have changed over time. These ultimate omnipotent beings are reflections of the populace who pray to them. These grand archetypes are given power through the human need for them. The founders of the United States and their hidden systems of beliefs through various occult organizations believed life was divine. It was that fact alone, they thought, that should be the basis for our need to be moral and just with a civilization of freedom and comradery. It could be said that it was Freemasonic ideals, which were also fostered and born out of the same age of renaissance and enlightenment that birthed other secret societies, that our nation's original ideals were directly influenced from.

What is important is that our awareness of these secret societies may be new and exciting, but they are not new or anything to be taken lightly. This knowledge, the truth of which I will discuss, has been around since the dawn of mankind and long before that. In our spoiled and advantageous generation, we relish in the results of men and women before us who sought ever higher in their motives to bring about elevated intellect and prosperity. Though humanity has had its disgusting moments of cruelty, something in us has perpetually pushed us to seek a more spiritual and meaningful existence.

Are we divine? Being divine implies that we are more than just carnal beings who have descended from apes. It means we have been deliberately created and for a greater purpose beyond this planet. Being divine means that our purpose transcends physical life and that our actions have consequences that can affect not just the life around us but even the celestial ecosystem we share a universe with. Divine doesn't necessarily mean good but simply that we have a creator and that we are granted our attributes and responsibilities from it.

The Anunnaki Theorem is the concept built from many scholars over the centuries, which postulates that all mythologies of the major world religions stem from a source, that source being the Sumerian Anunnaki mythos. I'll be diving into various mythologies and esoteric history to bring veracity to that theorem. Our ancestors believed life was divine, and that we are divine, that there was a deliberate act by someone to create us.

Since time immemorial mankind has dedicated sacred relics and sites to worship the divine. The divine, however, may be separate from the sanctified. That which exists outside of the influence of humanity is God. That which we give vain sacred power to, which in turn controls us is religion. Religion is an institution set up to control a narrative on the divine. As H. L. Mencken put it in his famous 1930s *On the Treatise of the Gods:*

"The essence of mysticism is that it breaks down all barriers between the devotee and his god, and thereby makes the act of worship a direct and personal matter. In theory, no ceremony is required, nor any priest, nor even any teacher. The mystic brings himself into contact with Omnipotence by any device which pleases his fancy and can be demonstrated to work in his case. He may resort to magical formulae, to narcotics, to violent physical activity, or to painful ascetic practices, or he may accomplish his purpose very simply by introspection and prayer. The main thing is that, without the aid of any human agent, he comes face to face with his god, and can make his wants known directly. The intervention of a liturgy, as of a priest, would be absurd ..."

Mencken brings up a great point in that mysticism or self-realization is what spiritualism is supposed to be about. It is a personal connection with the divine. The institution of religion today is the asinine construct that hides truth in plain sight to obfuscate it and control its effect. Most spiritual doctrines teach a basic belief that humanity derived from a deliberate creation and that we are trapped here and need to ascend back to that place of creation. Religion teaches us that we need to mediate this process with the priest and Church. Mysticism teaches us that this is an internal process that can be done by spiritual awareness.

In this book we'll go deeper into the origins of religion and the divine via the Sumerians and the cultures that immediately emerged after them. It is important to explore some of the other ancient belief systems that have influenced how we understand the divine also before investigating the Sumerian roots of modern religion.

Apart from the sacred writings of the Sumerian people, the oldest religious text we have are the Pyramid Texts from Egypt. They were written in Old Egyptian and carved on the walls and sarcophagi of the pyramids at Saqqara during the third millennium BCE. Old Egyptian refers to the archaic version of the later perfected Hieroglyphic system of Egypt. The construction of the texts, scholars say, was done under King Unas, the last pharaoh of the fifth dynasty. These texts contained Egypt's first expressions on the structure of the universe, the role of the gods, and the afterlife. These texts gave way to the later and more famous *Book of the Dead.* They were officially studied by French archaeologist and Egyptologist Gaston Maspero. After rumors that a local laborer curiously scouted the inside of one of the pyramids at Saqqara and found writings engraved on the walls, Maspero among other scholars had a piqued interest in the gossip. After some trouble and debate, Maspero was afforded oversight of excavating the sites. What was uncovered was about four thousand lines within several pyramids. The texts mention a plethora of gods with the most notable being Ra, Thoth, Osiris, and Isis. There are spells, incantations, and preparations for the passing of the king's soul to the afterlife. The center focus of the texts is the journey that the king's soul would undertake after his death. It was understood that the king had a right to join the gods in a sort of heaven that the Pyramid Texts endearingly calls "The Field of Reeds." It was there that the king would join the gods and live in eternal peace with them, still in a human body but one rid of sickness and death. The Egyptians believed in a *Ka*, a soul as we would know it. It was with this vehicle accompanied by the incantations of the Pyramid Texts, chanted by the priest, that the king would transition victoriously to the place of the gods also known as the place among the "Imperishable Stars." However, this journey was not a naive adventure. The soul had to pass through Osiris's Hall of Judgment. Not only was the soul judged upon its character once it passed on through the astral realm toward the "heaven," but it would also encounter evil spirits who would attempt to lead the consciousness astray. The process of preparing for the transition of death was imperative. Like falling asleep, if not focused strongly on the process of crossing over, one could lose themselves to the messy array of the other side.

The stories about the gods and creation from the ancient Egyptians changed throughout time, becoming more detailed and creative. The stages that their creation stories went through are individually titled by scholars as the Hermopolitan, Heliopolitan, Memphite and Theben theologies. Taking the various aspects of the creation story from each one and piecing it together we get a familiar story.

Told in short, it is said that in the beginning there was a watery darkness, a sort ethereal sea of blackened plasma. It was called the "waters of chaos." Within this matrix there was the first being Atum, who was meditatively apprehended in what is described as an egg-like pod. Atum was less of a corporeal creature and more of a force. Atum was androgenous, and because of this it created the first pair of beings, separating the creative male and female forces. From this pair the gods were born. Known as the Ennead, a total of ten familial gods with Horus being the later addition, earth began to be fashioned. Once the earth was fashioned there was a glorious time when only the gods existed, known as Zep Tepi. After this time of gods, humans were created. For some time, the gods and humans coexisted. After the gods grew old and weary the humans became bold. After attempting to rebel against and kill the god Ra, it was determined that the gods should leave earth. The gods, after killing many of the humans and sparing some, left toward the stars to then exist eternally in "heaven."

This story has symbology that we can see repeated in other cultures such as the beginning being of a watery chaos, which is how the later Hebrew Bible would also describe it. As we see here:

Genesis 1:2 KJV

"And the earth was without form, and void; and darkness was upon the face of the deep. And the Spirit of God moved upon the face of the waters."

There is also the concept of Atum having the ability to speak life into existence and manifest what it desires, which is precisely what the Old Testament declares about God. When the book of Genesis is accounting the days of creation it is remembered that God simply had to say, "Let there be light …" and light was created.

The power of the word is a reoccurring theme in esoteric ideology. Word is vibration accompanied by imagination; it intends to bring forth something from the mind into projection, into existence. In Hindu and Buddhist philosophy the Om or Aum mantra is a representation of God's essence. The sound, it is believed, is the infinite vibration that reverberates through all things, sustaining reality. Through the Aum chant, God manifested all life into existence. When chanting this in meditative prayer, one is attuning themselves with the creator of all, harmonizing with the universe.

Among the ancient belief systems, we also had Zoroastrianism. This foregone way of life contributed to the emergence of the dualistic concept of good and evil. It was this idea that eventually led to the notion that we must adhere to the source of good to escape the torment of a hellish desolation.

Zoroastrianism, known as Mazdayasna by its remaining followers, is a religion based on the teachings of Zoroaster. The date for its origins is unclear mostly because many of its writings were destroyed by Greek, Mongol and Arab invaders. Its legendary beginning goes all the way back to the second millennium BCE. The substantially agreed-upon date is around 600 BCE give or take some years. The central figure, Zoroaster, properly pronounced Zarathustra, was an Iranian prophet who was born into a noble family. By his early teen years, he was being educated by the priesthood. At the time Persia had a polytheistic belief system that conducted ritual animal sacrifice. This custom along with others inherently bothered Zarathustra. By the age of thirty Zarathustra had a vision by a river where a divine emissary manifested to him. This emissary claimed to be Vohu Mahah, sent from Ahura Mazda to declare to the prophet that there is but one God and he requires not archaic rituals but only a moral life apart from the practices his people were used to. The to-be prophet communed with the god Ahura Mazda on several occasions. It was this deity that would show Zarathustra the truth about life. The prophet became a reformer, traveling the lands preaching this new truth, which wasn't well received. He was exiled and threatened with death.

Although there is no evidence of his actual life, where the legend begins to merge with history is with the Persian Achaemenid Empire (550–330 BCE). It was king Cyrus II, Cyrus the Great, who first helped popularize Zoroastrianism across the Persian kingdom. Along with the Achaemenids the later Parthian and Sassanian Empires also further developed the religion of Zoroastrianism. It was in the early fourth century CE that the Sassanians officially wrote down the books of Zoroaster known as the Avesta. Prior to that time, most of the legend and sacred stories surrounding Zoroaster were passed down orally. Holding strong, eventually the old Persian Empire fell to Muslim conquest, reducing the Zoroastrians to a fraction of what they used to be.

Auguetil Duperron of Paris published the first European translation of the Avesta In 1771. It is a collection of legendary scriptures that were dictated by Ahura Mazda to Zarathustra. They are intended to be read as songs or meditative mantras. It is said that the original scriptures were written down on tablets of gold and were recited in prayer. It took Zarathustra over ten years to gain any converts, but he eventually won the faith of legendary king Vishtaspa, the first ruler to accept the new teachings. The king like Zoroaster is concluded as mythical, for there are no substantial pieces of evidence for his existence. The oldest parts of the Avesta are the Gathas, a section said to be writings and teachings directly from Zarathustra. The Gathas are the central core of the religion. They are the words of the prophet himself. The reverence for Ahura Mazda was so great that King

Darius I, third ruler of the Persian Achaemenid Empire, inscribed in a stone that can still be read today that:

"The great Ahura Mazda which is the greatest of the gods has made Darius king ... I am king through the gracious will of Ahura Mazda. O man think no evil. The command of Ahura Mazda is this: think nothing evil, leave not the right way, sin not ..."

Although Ahura Mazda was seen as the ultimate godhead by Zarathustra, this strict doctrine of monotheism wasn't adopted by the people or kingdom so quickly. Within the same inscription by Darius, he states:

"May Ahura Mazda grant me aid, together with the clan gods ..."

The goal of Zarathustra was to reform the polytheistic practices of his people and to purge them of the "sorcery" they were involved in. Pre-Zoroastrian Persia followed the beliefs of the Indo-Europeans.

The Indo-European culture was the progenitor of the English, Spanish, German, and Greek languages and religious texts. The origin of these people is speculated to have begun in Eurasia in the fourth millennium BCE. Spreading across to the various places that would spawn some of the major countries of today, they brought with them their mythologies. The primitive development of their belief system centered around pagan nature worship. Later, the different aspects of nature were fused with anthropomorphic deities. The tale of these gods consisted of adventures, wars and creation. Within these stories is a family of main characters who were the prototype for the later romanticized Greek and Roman gods. For example, the Hittites spoke of a "Storm God," who was their patron deity. In what is considered the oldest Indo-European text to date, the Anitta text, a famous Hittite king spoke of a deity titled "Siu-Summin." This roughly translates to "our god." Sius (god) is seen as an etymological root for the Indo-European word *dyeus*, which also became the Greek "Zeus" and Latin "Deus." The Hittites ruled over ancient Anatolia, modern-day Turkey, which is the landmass that sits directly to the right of the Greek island chains.

Among the various cultures that emerged from the Indo-Europeans were the Indo-Iranians. The oldest of their religious text is the Rigveda. The Rigveda is directly responsible for the beliefs of Pre-Zoroastrian Persia and that of modern-day Hinduism. Zoroastrianism texts still contain linguistic remnants of the Rigveda, such as names of certain deities. The Rigveda is the oldest of the Vedas, which is a total of four books that contain hymns to the gods and their escapades. The Rigveda being the oldest is said to have been written around 1700–1100 BCE. The oldest surviving manuscript dates to the eleventh century CE. There are commentaries on the scriptures going back to the second half of the first millennium CE. Just like the Avesta, the Rigveda was passed down orally until it was committed to writing by later priesthoods. The scriptures, like the later Avestan writings, are meant to be chanted and thought of as a vibrational message that harmonizes one with the creative source of the universe. The Rigveda's creation story again takes a similar approach to the Egyptian text and later Judaic scripture. The tale starts with a primordial nonexistence even speaking of "cosmic waters," the ethereal plasma that preceded the first being. As it beautifully declares in the passages of the Nasadiya Sukta:

"At first there was only darkness wrapped in darkness. All this was only unillumined water. That One which came to be, enclosed in nothing, arose at last, born of the power of heat."

Like the Egyptian creation myths, the first being in the Rigveda creates the sky and earth, which are expressed as sentient beings. The first being according to the Egyptian text was Atum; in the Rigveda he is known as Tvsatr. In the Egyptian story Atum creates the twin beings Shu and Tefnut who are described as two different aspects of air. These twins begin to create the other facets of the physical world, "separating the sky from the waters." These other characteristics, such as the dry land (Geb), are remembered as the first gods who comprise the physical reality we live in. The Hebrew Old Testament relates the same occasion in Genesis 1:6:

"And God said, Let there be a firmament in the midst of the waters, and let it divide the waters from the waters. And God made the firmament, and divided the waters which were under the firmament from the waters which were above the firmament: and it was so ..."—KJV

The Rigveda exalts a similar story claiming that after the cosmic waters Tvsatr is self-created, then the Earth and Sky, personified as beings, are also created. Both in the Egyptian and Indo-European cosmologies after the foundational elements of the universe are created, the corporeal archetypal gods are fashioned. Later, humanity is then created. Within the Rigveda there are numerous gods that are extolled and also demons that we are informed about. These beings are the Asuras also called Devas (gods). They're categorized under two different classes called the Adityas and the Danavas, the latter being the evil beings symbolized by serpent imagery and the Adityas being the benevolent ones represented by birds.

It was the worship and focus on these many deities that Zarathustra came to rectify. The bold conviction given by the prophet is that the prior Devas, which are presently worshipped as the good gods by Hindus, are evil and not to be trusted. Zarathustra continued to reverse certain practices of the archaic Persian beliefs as Bipin Shah states in his essay "Early Vedic Schism-Indo-Iranian Split and Rise of Zoroastrianism":

"'Rta' in Veda is the cosmic order of the universe, Asha is the falsehood, while in the Avesta, 'Asha' is literally 'truth' and foundation of order of universe, while 'Rta' is the falsehood."

For Zarathustra the only purpose in life was to praise Ahura Mazda (wise lord) with "Good Thoughts, Good Words, Good Deeds." Apart from this the believer must be aware of the opposing dark force Angra Mainyu, the sort of Satan figure that undermines Ahura Mazda's creation and leads the Devas to conduct distractions and obstacles for the good person. According to the Zoroastrians, in the beginning there existed both the light and dark forces independently from each other. Ohrmazd (Ahura Mazda) created the universe and placed it in an egglike containment. Ahriman (Angra Mainyu) crept into the realm and began dispelling his evil creations thus initiating the conflict between good and evil. To escape the snares of Ahriman the Zoroastrian must focus their lives toward Ohrmazd and willingly choose to subjugate themselves under him as the supreme God of all.

Ohrmazd did not act alone, however. He had seven divine beings who helped assist him in his endeavors who could also intervene on earth with humans. These beings are called the Amesha Spentas, the "good immortals." All the while Ahriman is creating havoc with his brigade of evil spirits, each person is given a choice to choose good or evil in the Zoroastrian religion. According to the doctrine, at the end of one's life they will face the "bridge of judgment" where they must eternally choose who to serve. The ideas of God versus Satan, the end of days along with a judgment, and a messianic anticipation in Judaism and Christianity can be surmised to have been influenced by Zoroastrianism. The Zoroastrian idea of the divine emissaries was also a forerunner for the later fortified angelology of Judaism.

Judaism, the major religion that spawned from the Israelites, is sometimes broken down into two historical sections, the pre-exilic era and the post-exilic era. The ancient Israel kingdom comprised of the northern kingdom of Israel and the southern kingdom of Judah. Around 700 BCE the north was sieged by the Assyrians. The humble kingdom of Judah was holding strong but faced the threat of the Assyrians, Egyptians and rising Babylonian Empire. Assyria began to arise fiercely under its last ruler, King Ashurbanipal, during the last half of the seventh century BCE. He managed to attack and take over parts of Egypt. This was all foreshadowing a day of reckoning for the small kingdom of Judah. One of the last hopeful reformers of Judah was king Josiah (640–609 BCE). He attempted to turn things around but could not. Along with him arose the famous prophets of the Old Testament, attempting to awaken the people to the danger that lay ahead. It was all to no avail; the people had lost their faithfulness and receded to idol worship and licentiousness. The Babylonians rose to power under Nabopolassar and defeated the Assyrians, seizing their properties. It was his son Nebuchadnezzar II who destroyed Judah and took the multitude of its royals into exile in Babylon in about 597 BCE.

Pre-exilic Judaism owes its origin to the native tribes of the ancient Palestinian area who worshipped a polytheistic council of gods. These gods were incorporated from the Canaanite religions. The first mention of the Israelite tribe derives from a stele erected around 1210 BCE by the Egyptian pharaoh Merneptah. In the stele the pharaoh boasted about his vanquish of a militaristic "tribe of Israel." World-renowned expert in the Hebrew Bible and professor at the College de France and the University of Lausanne, Thomas Romer, explains the Canaanite origins of Israel in his book *The Invention of God*. He explains that the native tribes of Israel assimilated the cult of Yahweh, the later transformed El, from the neighboring tribes in Canaan. El was the chief deity of the Canaanites. Early Judaism was polytheistic as Romer stated to Haaretz, "Jeremiah speaks about the many gods of Judah, which are as numerous as the streets of a town." It was this praising of many gods that the weak Judah would find trouble reconciling as the encroaching kingdom of Babylon began to take over the area. It wouldn't be until the post-Babylonian exile that the nation of Israel would unite under a single God, Yahweh. Eventually the Babylonian kingdom was defeated by the Persian kingdom under king Cyrus the Great. It was this king who would eventually liberate the captive Jews and allow them the choice to go back home. This is attested in the now "Cyrus Cylinder," a physical stone text written in Akkadian cuneiform found in 1879. In the cylinder, Cyrus boasts of the liberation of peoples and the returning of artifacts to their rightful place. It is this same king who is exalted in the Bible as being the one who freed the Jews from captivity. The Jews see the event from their perspective and call him the anointed by Yahweh, stating their God called upon him to help them in their endeavors. However, the Cyrus Cylinder makes it clear that Cyrus was loyal to Marduk, and Enlil, both gods with ancient roots in Sumer. He declares within the text:

"Marduk, the exalted, the lord of the gods, turned towards all the habitations that were abandoned and … he searched everywhere and then he took a righteous king, his favorite, by the hand, he called out his name: Cyrus, king of Ansan; he pronounced his name to be king all over the world … I am Cyrus, king of the universe, the great king, the powerful king, king of Babylon, king of Sumer and Akkad, king of the four quarters of the world …"

It's obvious he's not a worshipper of "God" in the Jewish sense of today. The dogmatic view of God today was not present then, not even among the Israelites; it was yet to be born. Cyrus was venerating gods and kingdoms of antiquity, which we will examine in detail in the next chapter.

When the Babylonians took Judah, as it was their custom, they only took interest in taking captive its elite. During the seventy years and through the Persian occupancy, it is assumed that many of the priests, scribes, scribes, prophets, and so on ... interacted with those of Babylon and Persia. Naturally, the Jewish elite grew interested and sympathetic to some of their philosophical ideas. Cyrus was tolerant of native religions and allowed his subjects to practice them freely. Although he wasn't apparently a Zoroastrian, it was a dominant belief within his kingdom. In this renaissance-like period where people were being liberated, we can imagine that there was an intrigue toward each other's culture.

It is said that once the Jews returned to their homeland, they brought back with them the fortified Judaism that would grow to be the one we are familiar with today. With this new religion, a truly monotheistic one, there arose new laws and philosophies. It was the Jewish priest of the Babylonian exile Ezra, with the help of Nehemiah, who would bring this reformed Judaism to Israel.

Ezra was commanded to read the reformed laws of Moses to the people, updating and conditioning them to the new way of life. He was sent to do this under the Persian king Artaxerxes, as is evident by the story in the Bible. Scholars still debate whether it was specifically Artaxerxes; however, it's agreed Ezra was sent after the Babylonian exile to indoctrinate the people into a new system of Jewish life. Many have concluded that Ezra was a high-ranking Jewish official within the Persian court who was appointed as a minister to teach these new laws, which the specific Jewish subjects under the kingdom would have to follow. J. Blenkinsopp in his *Persia and Torah*, where many similarities to Persian customs are examined, like many others concludes that the Torah as was being finalized during the years of Ezra and Nehemiah, was issued as a decree by the Persian Kingdom with heavy Zoroastrian influence.

"The fact that the Jewish law is the only one mentioned in the decree (Ezra 7:14, 21, 25) and that the penalties for infraction of the laws, listed in descending order of severity, are characteristic of Persian rather than Jewish penal practice, suggests the conclusion that the Jewish law Ezra was authorized to enforce is now invested with the authority of the monarch, and therefore is, in effect, royal Persian law as far as Jews in the satrapy are concerned."

The basic agreed-upon narrative is that Ezra, a Jewish scribe and official, was authorized by the Persian kingdom to organize and unify his people under a religious system so that they could be self-governed after the exile. This law with various hints of Zoroastrian influence was acceptable to the Persian kingdom and was not seen as a threat. This was a clever way to allow people to practice religious freedom while also keeping a local legal system cohesive with the wider kingdom to have the people self-governed.

As concluded by Dr. M. D. Magee in his *Ezra and Nehemiah: Bringing Judaism from Persia:*

"Jewish religion was created as a matter of imperial policy by the Persian Zoroastrian shahanshahs, but that inference draws closer once the shahs are seen to be interested in regulating local cults. Darius was furious that Gadatas, one of his officials in Ionia, had taxed the sacred gardeners of Apollo of Magnesia, despite his 'policy about deities.' Persian policy was to keep the priests of local cults on their side by allowing them taxation privileges ('ateleia') in return for keeping order—helping to collect taxes and enforcing the law through their cults."

Thus, it seems as though the need to create systems of religion despite their vast reasons are all human reasons. It's a part of our nature to organize, create systems, and then create symbols or dogma to represent the system that we place ourselves into for self-governance.

Divinity is usually regarded as the revealed motive for a religion and from there it takes on a human philosophy, which progresses into an institution, which contends with the neighboring beliefs for supremacy. Within all major religions there are similar ideas, or outright retold stories, and that is because we are one civilization on a considerably small planet. Our history is but one; we can only have one human creator but many religions. The confusion lies in whose version we listen to.

On the issue of God, the origins of the very word are complex. Its etymological formation primarily stems from the Proto-Germanic word *Gudan* or *Gud*, loosely meaning to invoke, spirit, or worship. These words trace back through the Indo-European languages to the Sanskrit Huta. Huta means "to give sacrifice to." In other words, praise or veneration. Following the line we find the root word *Gu*, which represents things with life-giving properties such as breasts, semen, sunrays, food, and so on. These life cycles were "good" and of "God." Along with these words we have the Persian *Kuta*, meaning master, guide, and inner knowledge. Before these we had the word *Gad*, used by the Phoenicians, meaning luck, fortune, or blessing. One of the furthest linguistic roots we can take this correlation is the African Buntu word *Gudu*, meaning sky or above. This is interesting because the head of the Sumerian pantheon, the oldest structure of gods known to us coming from a post-Paleolithic civilization, is Anu, which also means heaven or sky.

The point here is that we are dealing with many interpretations and translations, of what we might feel mean the same thing; however, if we aren't accurate in our speech, we might not be conveying the same thing. To speak of Anu would be directly invoking an ancient deity of Sumerian culture; this is not in line with the meditative idea of the "Creator." Anu was not the supreme creator of all; he was just a deity and even had to fight another one by the name of Alalu for the throne, as is made clear in a survived Hurrian text about the conflict, which can be read about in an essay published by E. A. Speiser titled "An Intrusive Hittite-Hurrian Myth." Speiser summarizes the story as follows:

"Long ago the god Alalu was king in heaven and Anu was his vizier. After nine years Anu turned on Alalu and drove him into the dark earth, himself becoming king in heaven ..."

The unknowable Creator of everything could never be justified in the name Anu. Just as when we speak of "God" in a Judeo-Christian sense we are calling upon a European translation of the many Hebrew terms that were used to call upon their deity within the Old Testament. The Jews didn't use the word God, they used what is known as the Tetragrammaton, the four letters of an unspeakable name rendered as YHWH. Aside from this name, the God of the Bible is also addressed by differing titles such as Adonai, El Shaddai, El, Elohim, and so on … When it comes to talking about "God" we might think we are all saying the same thing but unless we are, we might not be.

Despite the many religions and kingdoms that have existed throughout human history, we have always systematically thought of our universe as being deliberately created, which was followed by an era of gods, angels, and demons. By this concept we are divine; we were created with intention. This book as it will progress is not so much about proving that we were divinely created but rather that this is what we have told ourselves since the beginning of humanity and more importantly that the legends of this creation are variations fitting into a genre all of which were inspired and retold from an original source. That source is what I aim to investigate and present here in this work.

Chapter 2

Our Progenitors

With all the religions around the world contending for supremacy, it is paradoxical but reality to say, they are all right, yet they are all wrong. The relative and subjective nature of worship is what drives religious people to act upon what they believe are their spiritual duties. For the most part people are just following the customs of their family or culture. To tell them that their religion is wrong and some other person's religion on the other side of the world is right would be preposterous! The religions of the world fight and debate; they murder and heal all in the name of divinity. Strange religious sites in ancient ruins are visited by mystical seekers. The holy lands of the Near and Middle East are reverently fought over and visited by all walks of life. We all want to believe in some higher force. We all hope to come across some sign of the divine whether it be in our mind or at some ruin of an ancient site long gone. In one home one might be shouting out to a Hindu god, Christian god, Aztec god, and so on and so forth, but really, who's listening? Are there really that many gods existing and working to answer everyone's cries? Is there one God who watches over us all who knows how to speak every language or at least understand it? A technique I've used to get to the bottom and sift through all the lies and conditioning is what I call digging for the source. We must go to the source of all things. Only there lies the truth and even then, you'll be led further and further; it's all up to you when you want to stay content with where you are at in life. Are you content with going to church every Sunday, not reading the whole Bible yourself and letting another grown adult preach to you their interpretations of one of the most convoluted books of all time? Christianity, Islam, Judaism, Buddhism, Hinduism, and every other religion under the sun has a source. When considering the source, we see the reasoning for the conundrum at hand. Prior to all these named religions, there was a time when neither of them existed. As a matter of fact, there was a time when neither of those cultures and civilizations that worshipped thereof existed. Let us go back to the beginnings of humankind.

Mainstream academia will tell you that our specified "civilized" species of human dates to roughly six thousand years ago. That's puny. To think that everything we know and all that has ever occurred in our existence as a civilized human race has happened within six thousand years is extraordinary. Early Homo sapiens go back about 300,000 years and yet suddenly out of nowhere we sprung up and started creating a full-fledged civilization around 5000 to 4000 BCE. From being "simple" agricultural people to flying rockets, performing genetic engineering, and creating simulated realities, we've become a whole new being, unrecognizable from our humble animal-like past as early hominids. Another strange thing about us is that we still do not know where our current species of human stems from and that has led to the great "missing link" debate. Scientists and scholars alike have tried to pinpoint how we went from Neanderthal to Homo sapiens. As it stands it is as if we are two totally different creatures. The scope of this drastic change from caveman to a highly advanced and conscious modern human was as rapid as an overnight change in the grand scope of life. It was as if something or someone interjected and deliberately created the change. Mainstream academia will have you believe that we stemmed from evolutionary processes. These processes can be described as us beginning as beastly amphibious creatures evolving to upright simians to now civilized, thinking sapiens. The other half of humanity will tell you we stemmed from God, gods, and the rest alike. How did we emerge? Well, what did our ancestors think? The ones who must have witnessed the beginning?

In the 1800s a place in the Middle East was uncovered beneath the sands of time. It was uncovered by adventurous men such as J. S. Buckingham and Sir

Henry Layard. This enigmatic and miraculous place would later be known as Sumer, home of the Sumerians.

In the early 1800s the Ottoman provinces of the modern-day Near East, Syria, Palestine, and Iraq became more open to foreign travelers. J. S. Buckingham claimed to be the first person in over a century to write about his journey there in 1827. Buckingham respectfully wore Arab garb to mix in with the locals to go about his excavating and studying without conflict. This practice was made custom to some of the later explorers such as the famed pioneer Assyriologist who would follow fifty years later, Austen Henry Layard. As Westerners began to flock into the area, starting with the affluent buying property, eventually areas of historical interest began to be claimed by the Europeans. During the nineteenth century archeological sites began to be erected; the Germans at Assur and Babylon, the French at Khorsabad, and the British under Layard at Nineveh. What was found were massive collections of pottery, statues, figurines, tablets with fascinating writings, temples, burials; an entire civilization lost to us. It was apparent then as it is now that Sumer was the birthplace of all civilization. The Sumerians left behind massive temples with unprecedented archeology engineered with measurements and alignments toward celestial respects. In a light scientific online paper by William F. Romain titled "Lunar alignments at Ur: Entanglements with the Moon God Nanna," we learn that the Ziggurat of Ur, Sumer's most prized temple standing at one hundred feet tall, is aligned toward the moon's north horizon. This is done so accordingly to the worship of a later lunar deity known as Nanna. The Sumerian formed the first basic government, education systems, agriculture, mathematics, geometry, arts, astrology, mythology, literature, language, and intricate writing styles. They accomplished so many astonishing firsts as a civilization some might see as being less advanced than us. Among their many righteous works was an intricate record-keeping of knowledge. Their writing style, known as cuneiform, was a strange style created by using a wedge-shaped stylus on wet clay that was later baked and hardened. On their cuneiform tablets they inscribed infinitely valuable information.

Sumerian writing started off as glyphs similar to the Egyptian hieroglyphs, then over thousands of years those glyphs were changed to a quickened style of representing them through the cuneiform script. Their strange alien-like writing style was difficult to decipher. It was made possible by a fortunate find of a trilingual text made by King Darius (522–486 BCE) in Eastern Iran. Also known as the Behistun text, the inscription details a victory made by King Darius in Old Persian, Babylonian and Elamite, all relatives of the ancient Sumerian text and language. From these old-world languages, we were able to patiently trace back signs, syllables, and whole words to Sumerian. Also important to the decipherment was the fact that Sumer and Akkad, being sister empires, had their students learn each language and writing system. We have since found dictionaries of Akkadian and Sumerian words. Because Akkad's writing and culture were similar to the later Babylon, once we understood Babylonian writing, jumping to Akkad we were able to eventually decipher Sumerian. The decipherment through the Behistun Inscription began with Henry Rawlinson, in the mid-nineteenth century, taking paper prints of the text back to England, setting off the race to decipher Sumerian. Prior to Rawlinson, Georg Friedrich Grotefend, a German epigraphist and philologist, in 1802, was the first to decipher the Old Persian portion, giving a starting advantage to the later Assyriologists. Reverend Edward Hincks, a part of the initial translators of cuneiform, was later employed by the British Museum to work on deciphering texts. He was brilliant and able to decipher at a genius level. His papers were left at the museum from which later eager Assyriolgist Sir Henry Rawlinson glanced over and used to his advantage to publish his works off. Henry Rawlinson, according to modern master of Assyriology Irving Finkel, who is also

Assistant Keeper of Ancient Mesopotamian script, languages, and cultures in the Department of the Middle East in the British Museum, was a sort of scammer who plagiarized his career from the work of Hincks. Finkel recounts in his live presentation for the Royal Institution titled "Cracking Ancient Codes …," that when Rawlinson was an old man, he was asked how he deciphered cuneiform to which he replied, "I don't remember." It was Hincks who realized that there were other texts in the southern Babylon area that were written in cuneiform that did not belong to the Semitic language of Assyrian or Babylon. Cuneiform is a writing style, whereas the language that was spoken by the peoples of the trilingual Behistun text was Semitic, relating to modern Hebrew. But there were other texts that did not seem to be culturally related to these Semitic texts. Among the early translators there was the hopeful French Assyriologist Jules Oppert, who suggested calling these peoples the Sumerians, based on inscriptions that read "King of Sumer and Akkad." Samuel Noah Kramer, famed twentieth-century Assyriologist, credited Hincks, Rawlinson and Oppert as the "holy triad" of cuneiform decipherment. Thus once they were able to decode the Behistun Inscription, they would leave the way to decipher the cuneiform of Sumerian.

The Sumerians, the progenitors of all civilization with a mythology and cosmology predating all other religions, accredited their whole existence to the Anunnaki. Anunnaki means "Those whom from Heaven to Earth came" as some have translated. Anu is the name of the head deity of the Sumerian pantheon, but it is also the word for sky or heaven. *Ki* is their word for earth but is also the name of the goddess Ki. Anunnaki can also be translated as royal offspring or bloodline. The term could be translated as the offspring of these two deities Anu and Ki. In the more speculative circles of scholars the term can be translated as a race of beings who descended here from the skies long ago.

This translation was made popular by the extensive researcher and writer Zecharia Sitchin in his famous *Earth Chronicles*, a series of books, started in the 1970s that present a detailed explanation of this theory. The earliest known use of the term Anunnaki comes from the writings of the Sumerian king Gudea (ca. 2144–2124 BCE). The Gudea cylinder seals, discovered in 1877 by French archeologist Ernest Choquin de Sarzec, tell of a group of deities known as the Anunnaki. They are also titled the "Seven gods who decree": An, Enlil, Enki, Ninhursag, Nanna, Utu, and Inanna. In the tale, Gudea is instructed by the gods to build a temple, which will be used for the gods. During the process the gods show admiration for Gudea's accomplishments. It is to be understood by the text that the gods are corporeal and involved in mankind's affairs. The Babylonian king of the second century BCE Hammurabi, revered the Anunnaki. He is taught in schools to be remembered as one of the first law givers or kings to construct a modern system of law. This law is known as the Code of Hammurabi. What is interesting is that he opens up the decree by showing respect to the gods as saying:

"When Anu the Sublime, King of the Anunaki, and Bel, the lord of Heaven and earth, who decreed the fate of the land, assigned to

Marduk, the over-ruling son of Ea, God of righteousness, dominion over earthly man, and made him great among the Igigi, they called Babylon by his illustrious name, made it great on earth, and founded an everlasting kingdom in it, whose foundations are laid so solidly as those of heaven and earth; then Anu and Bel called by name me, Hammurabi, the exalted prince, who feared God, to bring about the rule of righteousness in the land, to destroy the wicked and the evil-doers; so that the strong should not harm the weak; so that I should rule over the black-headed people like Shamash, and enlighten the land, to further the well-being of mankind."—translated by L. W. King

This is extraordinary praise by Hammurabi, showcasing the importance of the Anunnaki even then within the second millennium BCE. These deities of Heaven are interpreted by conspiratorial forums as an advanced race of sentient beings from afar. Is that not what every other religion has been trying to dogmatically claim as well? That some being or beings from the sky have partaken in our creation and world affairs?

What is left from Sumerian knowledge is grand. We are told that after the Gods ruled among themselves there was a period of the first human kings, as attested in the "Sumerian King List" wherein it states:

"After the kingship descended from heaven, the kingship was in Eridug (Eridu) …"

The gods passed on the responsibility of rulership to humans, to our earliest of ancestors. This list provides eight legendary rulers who ruled for a total of about 241,200 shars. These kings ruled "before the flood." Following after them are the remaining rulers with the totality of time spanning around 432,00 shars. Some more controversial scholars on the subject, like Sitchin, take a "shar" to mean years. More conservative and logical scholars see the divine shar as meaning days. For example, the first ruler, Alulim, ruled for 28,800 shars. This amount of time would be astronomical and impossible. The Sumerian mathematical system was based on sixty. If we take the shar to mean a divine year, which for them would be 360 days, then this would make more sense. If we divide 28,800 by 360 days, then that would mean Alulim ruled for a total of eighty years. Very normal and believable. One version of the Sumerian King List is inscribed onto a rectangular prism from the third millennium BCE. The first eight kings were legendary rulers before the "flood." At the end of the chronology of the first eight the text claims, according to Oxford's online translation: "In 5 cities 8 kings; they ruled for 241200 years. Then the flood swept over." Of course, the flood being referred to is the biblical or Sumerian flood story. Another source for this number comes from the Babylonian priest Berossus. Living and writing in the third century BCE, Berossus wrote books on the history of his people for the Greeks. His works were used as authoritative literature of history by later Greeks. His original writings only exist in fragments, translations and mentions in other works. Berossus also calculated that the legendary list of Sumerian rulers goes back to the enigmatic 432,000 shars.

The Sumerian tale of creation is composed in the "Enuma Elish" (When in the Heights). It's a Babylonian tale, which we can assume was passed down from the older Mesopotamian civilizations because of its Sumerian loan words. This creation story used to be acted out in a yearly play during the Babylonian New Year festival known as Akitu. It reads like an epic battle between gods, but it can be interpreted as the chaotic formation of our current solar system with its planets stationed in their respective orbits, with the planets in the story being reimagined as gods. This theory was made famous, again, by Zecharia Sitchin the writer on speculative Assyriology as I would title him. His theories have been widely debated and refuted by mainstream scholars; however, I think he provided some unique and risky insights into what our ancestors might have been telling us. In his *Genesis Revisited* he takes a deeper look at the Enuma Elish. The text opens up like all the other sacred cosmologies do that I have already gone over. In the beginning there was a sort of void followed by a mixing of waters. As translated in L. W. King's 1902 *Enuma Elish: The Seven Tablets of Creation* the opening line goes as follows:

"When in the Height Heaven was not named and the Earth beneath did not yet bear a name ..." There was the primeval "Apsu" and the mother of the gods "Tiamat ... Their waters mingled together ..."

After this mingling of waters, a series of divine couples were born starting with Lahmu and Lahamu. The surviving text is broken but it is assumed that there were about three pairs of couples making about six deities. Along with the six there were Apsu, Tiamat and the smaller assistant deities Mummu, Gaga, and Kingu all together eleven deities with the protagonist Marduk making the grand twelfth member. The story goes on to tell of a battle between Tiamat and the divine couples, her offspring. Apsu is distraught about the entire ordeal and is frequently consulting Mummu about the situation. As the war heads on, Tiamat grants Kingu the power to lead an army of eleven monsters against her chaotic offspring the three divine couples. In the end an outsider, in this case named Marduk (sometimes changed depending on the culture), enters the battles scene, fights back against Tiamat and her forces, eventually destroying her. Upon his victory Marduk cuts Tiamat in half. One of her halves became a sort of "firmament" separating her waters, as is seen in L. W. King's 1902 translation:

"He split her up like a flat fish into two halves; One half of her he established as a covering for heaven … not to let her waters come forth …"

Zecharia Sitchin sees all of this as being a metaphorical tale about our solar system being created. In his *Genesis Revisited* he details how the three couples are the six outer planets and that Apsu is the sun, Mummu-Mercury, and Tiamat was a huge legendary watery planet. When Tiamat was broken in half, during this chaotic time period in our solar system's past, one half became the asteroid belt and the other half-earth. His explanation is fascinating and draws some convincing conclusions, but they are not accepted in mainstream Assyriology.

Interestingly, in the early 1900s Reverend A. E. Whatham compared the similarities to the Enuma Elish story of Tiamat with the opening events in Genesis of the Old Testament. In his essay titled "The Yahweh-Tehom Myth," Whatham reveals that the word used in Genesis for the darkness or abyss in which God begins to create, *Tehom*, is a cognate of the Mesopotamian *Tiamat*. As he explains:

"After first creating light, Yahweh next proceeds to subdue, or bring under control, the surging waters of the turbulent abyss. He then divides it into two portions, making of the one the upper, and of the other the lower ocean. To keep the upper waters in their place, he creates a domelike support, rakia, correctly rendered in all our versions 'firmament.'"

Whatham declares that the rendering of Tiamat to Tehom was a deliberate exaltation of the Judaic religion or peoples over the gods and myths of the past. The Hebrew scribes were acknowledging the gods of the past such as the valiant Marduk and asserting their Yahweh as the new and ultimate victor over the chaotic forces of nature. The major religions of today have unfolded from the ancestorial past; although they at times pridefully claim to be original and untouched by any outside influence, that simply is not the truth.

Relaying back to Sitchin and his perspective on the Enuma Elish, he believed that the hero in the story, Marduk, was originally named Nibiru "Planet of the Crossing." This term is used in the Enuma Elish as a title after Marduk subdues Tiamat. This can be seen in Alexander Heidel's translation from his 1942 *Babylonian Genesis*. From lines 128–133 we read:

"Nibiru, the star that shines in the skies …

May he uphold the course of the stars of heaven;

May he shepherd all the gods like sheep;

May he subdue Tiamat, may he distress and shorten her life!"

Because of the metaphorical reference to Marduk as a star that shines in the skies, Sitchin asserted that the Enuma Elish was detailing how a specific planet was the cause for the creation of our solar system. He declared that it was also the home planet of the Anunnaki and that when it brushed up against our solar system, the basic biological life forms on those celestial bodies mixed together, seeding what would become life on earth and life on Nibiru. This planet, setting the solar system in its stationary position that it is in now, would be destined to return every 3,600 years, as it was incidentally caught in a long elliptical orbit, married to our star system. Sitchin believed that it was this myth and the Anunnaki that all other religions gained their stories and beliefs from and that even the cross was an ancient symbol for Nibiru. This is all fascinating conjecture but as we read in

Heidel's translation, Nibiru was one out of about fifty different titles that were given to the victorious Marduk, a custom of Sumer. Each god held a rank of sixty, fifty, or forty names depending on their status. Another name he was given, for example, was Pagalguenna, "the first of all the lords, the gods, the one whose strength is mighty ..."

Our history here on earth is vast and intriguing. When we look around and consider what we are a part of, we can realize that we are a body with a consciousness, living in an ecosystem on a considerably small planet within the outskirts of a huge galaxy. The bright and shiny thing that wakes us up every morning is not a burden; it is a star, a glorious one with wisdom much greater than any of us could imagine. Being able to traverse space whether by interplanetary vessels or by some advanced zero-point energy isn't impossible; it just hasn't been done yet by us at least. The knowledge of our past is mysterious, and we'd be arrogant not to pay attention to what our ancestors have tried to relay to us through their sacred writings.

The Sumerians, the first civilization with unbelievable advancement and no definitive genetic relation to the caveman, accredited their whole existence to the Anunnaki. When piecing together Sumerian tablets with contemporary texts the truth then merges. We are told in the Enuma Elish and also in the Enki and Ninmah tablet that labor on earth was originally taken care of by the lower-ranking deities. When the work became too much for the Anunnaki to bear, because of rebellion, the task to appease the mission was at hand. What ensued would be the most important occurrence for them and us. After council meetings it was decided by the chief Sumerian gods, Enki, Enlil, and Ninmah, with the approval of their father Anu, that a worker race of beings was to be genetically fashioned. It was not an easy task nor a widely accepted one. Enki, lord of earth and Ninmah, Mother goddess or goddess of life, were chosen for the task. According to Sitchin the task was accepted by Enki because he was especially aware of a sentient being that was fit to be genetically upgraded and this being was our primitive ancestor the "caveman." Sitchin believed that Enki and his team took the caveman and experimented with it until through trials of error a primitive worker was fashioned. This worker was created solely for the purpose of working under Anunnaki control. In a bilingual Sumerian-Akkadian text titled "The Creation of

Humankind," humans are made from the blood of the gods solely for the purpose of laboring for the gods, maintaining agriculture, irrigation and to celebrate the gods through worship. As is seen in a translation here:

"Let us create humankind from their blood. Their labor shall be labor for the gods; To maintain the boundary ditch for all time, To set the pickaxe and workbasket in their hands, To make the great dwelling of the gods, Worthy to be their sublime sanctuary … For celebrating the gods' festivals as they should …"

In the various Sumerian texts involving our creation, the mixing of Anunnaki blood is used to produce us. To Sitchin what we are reading is a crude explanation of genetic engineering. The ancient Mesopotamian texts speak of the Anunnaki deliberately creating mankind through a mixing of blood and clay. This is all reminiscent of the biblical story of God creating man out of clay and breathing life into him, animating his consciousness into existence. This idea too is seemingly influenced by the Sumerian creation tales as well.

Gleaning from Oxford's online corpus of Sumerian tablet translations, we find in the tablet known as "Enki and Ninmah," a similar event. After Enki is pressured to create a surrogate being to take over the work of the lower-ranking gods, he calls for several goddesses to help gather clay from the legendary Abzu and to knead the new being into existence. The Abzu was a primordial hidden palace that Enki resided over, usually thought to have been somewhere in southern Africa. During their trials, both Enki and Ninmah mistakenly created deformed and disabled humans until they finally perfect their design. Thus, in the Mesopotamian view of creation, mankind was created to help the gods and serve them. In a 2020 paper for the City University of New York (CUNY) titled "Adam and the Early Mesopotamian Creation Mythology," Saad D. Abulhab relates how the Quran also mentions that Adam was born of a mixture of divine blood as follows:

"The Hebrew Genesis was solidly clear that Adam was not only created with the blood of a god but he also had the look and feel of a god. Current translations of line 1:26 in Genesis claim it said 'Let us make man in our image, after our likeness.'* However, while the first relevant Hebrew word in the line, bi- ṣalamnū, correctly meant 'in our image,' the second word, ka-damwutnū, could not have meant 'as our likeness.' Surely, the word dumyatu can mean 'image' in old Arabic and Hebrew, and one can hypothesize it could also mean 'likeness,' but using two words with identical meanings after each other would be an unneeded repetition. This word was clearly related to the root Arabic words damū and damā, meaning blood. Therefore, ka-damwutnū can either mean 'as our blood' or 'as a piece of our blood.'"

Both the Islamic and Judaic mythologies involving the creation of man have obvious precedents in the very ancient Sumerian version going back at least a couple of thousand years before the Old Testament was put together. The human prototype created by the Sumerian gods was granted the gift and privilege of having Anunnaki genes that provided high levels of awareness. Apart from being made to be a worker for the gods, it is apparent that our human ancestor was cultivated into the self-aware and righteous being that would become the Homo sapiens race. In Sumerian lore we are told a tale about the first civilized human by the name of Adapa. Adapa has been attributed as a precursor to the biblical Adam. As I'll show, some of the gods were resentful for making mankind too evolved. This sentiment is reflected

in the Bible. God in the Bible was nervous about

mankind knowing too much as is seen in Genesis 3:22

and onward:

22 And the Lord God said, "The man has now become like one of us, knowing good and evil. He must not be allowed to reach out his hand and take also from the tree of life and eat and live forever."

23 So the Lord God banished him from the Garden of Eden to work the ground from which he had been taken.

24 After he drove the man out, he placed on the east side[a] of the Garden of Eden cherubim and a flaming sword flashing back and forth to guard the way to the tree of life.

This is an interesting show of God's vulnerability and

anthropomorphic nature. Again, we see a precedent for

this motif in Sumerian mythology. In the "Tale of

Adapa" we are told that after Adapa broke the wing of a

royal bird known as the "South Wind," he was called by

his creators in judgment to account for his actions. The South Wind it can be assumed was a huge monstrous mythical bird and for Adapa to be able to break its wing would have shown great power. Adapa was a wise and righteous man among his peers. As Fred Gladstone Bratton details in his translation from his 1970 *Myths and Legends of the Near East*, Adapa was a beloved man of the people with the intelligence of a god. After his destructive behavior, he is called to appear in front of Anu, the leading deity among the Anunnaki. Enki, Adapa's creator, prepares him for the meeting. As Enki, known as Ea in the tale, prepares Adapa by giving him special instructions on how to conduct himself, he also deceives Adapa. Enki knows that Anu will offer Adapa the drink of food of eternal life, but Enki doesn't want Adapa to be given eternal life for he is already a strong and wise being; this could mean that Adapa would become a god and a contender with the Anunnaki. So, Enki lies to Adapa and tells him that the food and drink are poison and a ploy by Anu to kill him, so if he is offered the sustenance he should respectfully refuse. Adapa gains the respect of the two Anunnaki who escort him to Anu, Gishzida and Tammuz who would later help defend his case. As Adapa clarifies his actions to Anu, the two gods step in to defend him as a righteous and pious human. Anu is impressed and decides to forgive Adapa, and just as Enki suspected, offers Adapa the food and drink of the gods, which would grant him eternal life. Adapa refused the drink; however, Anu still granted Adapa a long and healthy life free of all ills and sicknesses experienced by a regular human. Adapa returns to earth a mortal but a special one at that. Bratton, like many scholars, realized that this was an obvious precursor to the biblical Adam and the Forbidden Tree of the Knowledge of Good and Evil. He states in the opening of his translation:

"The Hebrew legend of the eating of the Forbidden Tree of knowledge and its implications of the origin of sin is thought to have come from the Adapa myth … Ea's deceitful advice is given to Adapa because he does not want his protege to become a full-fledged god …"

These are Sumerian tales of which we still have very little knowledge compared to the vast amounts of tablets that have yet to be deciphered and the ones we've lost to time. According to an article for BBC's *Machine Minds* in 2018, Sophie Hardach detailed that within the 150 years of the various cuneiform scripts being found, only about 10 percent have been deciphered. There are over tens of thousands held in different collections around the world.

Irving Finkel and his team at the British Museum oversee about 130,000 tablets. It's been estimated that at least 500,000 if not more than 1,000,000 Mesopotamian tablets have been uncovered by modern archeologists over the many decades. It takes wisdom and devoted studying to seek the knowledge and piece it together. When we compare Sumerian knowledge and divine tales from cultures and religions that followed, we see why all religions are so similar in their tales and symbols. That is because they stemmed from Sumerian mythology. A somewhat obvious rendering of the polytheistic belief of the Sumerian into the monotheistic religion of Judaism appears in Genesis 1:26. In English versions of the Bible, the verse is found to say, "And God said, let us make man in our image, after our likeness." Why are there plural words? Who is God talking to when he says, "Let _us_" and "after *our* likeness?" Some religious people will say that it is so because he was speaking to the angels or his son, Jesus Christ. The truth about the plural context is that this verse is one of the most critically mistranslated verses in the Old Testament. When the translators left the plural context, they fortunately left truth seekers a very important clue into the ancient past. The translators were missing important contextual knowledge about the pre-Judaic world and myths. The verse in its original Hebrew reads as "And the Elohim said, let us make man in our image ..." Elohim is a plural word, basically meaning multiple gods. Malbim, Russian-born rabbi and scholar of Hebrew who lived from 1809–1879, is remembered in Jewish academia as a prolific philosopher and writer on Jewish texts. His commentaries were the most popular in his day and regarded as authoritative. It was his works that would actually influence Zecharia Sitchin on the idea of the Anunnaki being a race of extraterrestrial god-men that came here long ago seeding civilization. Malbim's interpretation of the Elohim was that they were powerful beings. This makes etymological sense if El means powerful or god then Elohim would mean powerful ones or godly ones. In an online data sheet for Jewish scripture website Sefaria.org, put together by Geo Poor, titled "Evolution of an Idea: The Fallen Ones Session 2," Poor quotes Malbim as saying:

Who were the Bnei Elohim?

"They are the ones that it's said they fell from Heaven … it is known that in all the ancient stories of the nations they told that in the early days of the king over the kingdom, Bnei Elohim came down from the Heavens to the Earth and ruled over it and married women from the Bnot Adam, and to them were born strong, revered, perfect princes. Similar stories are found with the first kings of Egypt and Greece, which began from gods and half gods that walked on high mountains. And the stories say that they were wonderful and strong ..."

Here we see a very crucial distinction made by Malbim. Although in his other writings he declares that these Elohim were not to be worshipped and the concept of them bred false idols, he recognizes that this idea of powerful beings descending onto the earth and mating with our women was a legend basically taught by all major religions, stemming far back in time. Being that he was alive during the nineteenth century, Malbim couldn't have known in full about the Sumerian connection, and therefore didn't know that he was speaking truth when he said that this idea wasn't original to Judaism but stretched far back in time. This idea is indeed deeply rooted in our ancestorial legends, of course stemming from the Sumerian Anunnaki. The translators of the English Bible changed Elohim to God in confusion over the lost meaning. What they failed to change were the other plural words. Thankfully they did not because it is a small glitch in the matrix that leads to a valley of discovery. The Elohim then were the Anunnaki simply renamed and envisioned by modern man. Many cultures around the world have borrowed, exaggerated, and added to Sumerian knowledge. That is because our true past is deeply rooted and embedded in us if not through all the blatant rehashing of legends, then through the genetic and ethereal memory of what we are. The Anunnaki theory does not start there, however, but it starts with this. If all civilizations followed thereafter and borrowed their teachings and religious doctrines then that would mean that all religions when speaking about angels, demons, God, gods, or any being of that matter that had to do with our creation is referring to the Sumerian knowledge of the Anunnaki. That means that if taken for face value, we were deliberately created by a highly advanced race of beings akin to us. As the Bible states we were made in the image of the "Elohim." Their mission became ours and under them we labored and worshipped, gave thanks and praise. The Anunnaki theory can be simply described as this: the theory that proclaims all major Abrahamic and polytheistic religions and cultures around the world are renditions of the Sumerian culture and knowledge; that the idea of an anthropomorphic family of divine beings stems directly from the Sumerian Anunnaki.

Chapter 3

Their Remains

I can still remember the first time the fire inside of me for knowledge was sparked. It was a normal Thursday in first grade; we were off to the library to pick out a new book to read for the week. As usual I lingered in the history section flipping through dinosaur books with detailed and awesome descriptions and images. There was one for whatever reason that also mentioned knights and how they were said to have fought dragons. In one page about the knights, the writer also snuck in some knowledge about the "Holy Grail" and how knights were after it. I thought it was exactly that, a golden cup. The thought of it all mystified me and I wanted to find and drink from that super expensive cup. However, any learned scholar on the subject of the Holy Grail knows that it is not a cup at all but allegedly a complex representation of the lineage of Jesus Christ that the Knights Templar and such were commanded to secure. This theory was made famous by the 1983 book *Holy Blood, Holy Grail*. The authors proposed that the Holy Grail, usually thought to be the cup Jesus drank from at the Last Supper, was actually a code word for the lineage of Jesus Christ. They theorized that Jesus and Mary Magdalene had a romantic relationship and through them a secret family and lineage were conceived. It is said that through this line was born the mysterious Merovingian dynasty of Europe, hundreds of years later in the fifth century. The Merovingian kings never associated themselves with Christ and were in fact pagan by default. According to the seventh-century *Chronicle of Fredegar*, Merovech, the king whom the lineage was named after, was divinely conceived after his mother was impregnated by a "sea creature." Famous "Grail" legends go back to the twelfth century starting with Chrétien de Troyes. As Graham Hancock chronicles in his 1992 *The Sign and the Seal*, de Troyes began the fascination with the Grail in his unfinished work *Parzival*. The story follows an Arthurian character named Parzival who sets out to find the Holy Grail. Later writers would add on to the famous tale initiated by de Troyes. Wolfram von Eschenbach's *Parzival* became the climatic literary completion of the ongoing legend. Hancock theorized in his book that the fascination with the Holy Grail and biblical artifacts was sparked during the early Christian crusades to the holy lands that were then under Muslim control. After the knights of the crusades had secured the land, they found artifacts and documents that held sacred information. Conspiracy researchers have concluded that the Knights Templar were initiated by mystics of the land and shown mysterious artifacts, which led to them turning from the Church and practicing a more esoteric form of Christianity. This independence is thought to have led to their rapid downfall after the French monarch had ambushed, arrested, and killed many of the Knights Templar including their last leader, Jacque DeMolay, in 1314. Hancock speculated that the "grail mysteries" were written during the onset of Christianity's reclaiming of the land because they had stumbled upon some ancient and remarkable information that needed to be passed down in secrecy. Hancock concluded that the Holy Grail was a code word for the mysterious "Ark of the

Covenant," which was a powerful treasure chest with divine attributes, mentioned in the Bible.

Whatever the truth, I bring this up to show how pervasive esoteric knowledge of our past has been in our modern world. I was a young child then, reading that book about the Grail, with no real grasp on history but there I was faced with a tiny glimpse into the hidden knowledge of our past. I don't doubt that whatever conspicuous adult snuck that part into the children's book did so unintentionally. The relation that the Holy Grail mysteries have to the Anunnaki is that Christianity is wholly based on the fact that Christ was of the line of David. The Bible stressed the importance of Christ or the Messiah having to be of a specific bloodline. The entire Bible from beginning to end chronicles a genealogy, starting with Adam. If we are to understand that the Old Testament was influenced by the Sumerian tales, then this bloodline would be incidentally connected to the Anunnaki and could still be alive and well today. In this chapter I will mostly go over why we won't find any Anunnaki here with us, in the way our ancestors knew them. I'll speculate as to why, if the gods were real, they are not to be found. All we have left of them are tales and strange monuments.

The knowledge of our hidden past is old, and we must respect that at the time of our birth there were already aged and renowned men and women who were decades ahead of us in esoteric knowledge. We are simply catching up as mature adults and there is an incredible amount to catch up on. Since the time that I read that book on the knights as a child, a part of me has always been looking into the mysteries of the past.

Around the world, unnerving monuments of the past stand firm and stare us into the eyes with noble and deified posture. Exquisite divine works of architecture and engineering stand as a testament to time. The ancient builders and sculptures of such architecture are mysterious and fascinating. There are pyramids and temples all around the world with similar building styles. We take time from our lives just to go marvel at them. Many of the ancient structures around the world cannot be explained; their engineering is seemingly impossible with modern technology to replicate. They define our spiritual advancement. We feel as though we will never understand the wondrous works of the past, as though we will never be able to achieve their equivalency.

The Great Pyramids of Giza have at times been correlated with the gods of the past. Still baffling scientists to this day, mainstream academia tells us that the pyramids were built during the Old Kingdom of Egypt during the fourth dynasty, starting with Sneferu in 2613 BCE. Sneferu's pyramid, known as the Bent Pyramid, isn't a true pyramid but a failed attempt at one. It is located in Dashur, twenty-five miles south of Cairo. Its slope begins to rise at a triangular angle but instead of achieving the difficult engineering of having the slopes completely triangular, flat, and uniform all the way up, it caves inward halfway at a forty-three-degree angle, giving it a rounded bent look. The Great Pyramids are angled at about fifty-one to fifty-two degrees. Modern Egyptologists suggest that this pyramid is a prototype of the later Great Pyramids of Giza. Zecharia Sitchin, the prolific speculative Assyriologist, postulates in his *The Stairway to Heaven* that the reason Sneferu's pyramid was a failed attempt wasn't that it was a prototype later perfected by the Great Pyramids but a failed attempt at trying to mimic the already existing pyramids at Giza. The earliest Western source available to us about the construction of the pyramids at Giza comes from Herodotus in his *Histories*. He claimed that it took one hundred thousand slaves about twenty years to build the largest pyramid in Giza. It was also Herodotus who relayed that it was designed and constructed by the pharaoh Khufu. The two smaller were said to have been constructed by the following successors of the fourth dynasty, Khafre and nkaure. No one can conclude exactly how they were built, when they were built, how long it took or why they were built. The early theory that the pyramids were used as burial tombs has been long debunked. To this day no sarcophagi, mummies or extensive hieroglyphs have been found in the Great Pyramids. In Sitchin's book we find a quote from James Bonwick, a nineteenth-century historian pondering this mystery:

"Who can persuade himself that the Egyptians would have left such superb monuments without at least hieroglyphical inscriptions—they who were profuse of hieroglyphics upon all the edifices of consideration?"

What Sitchin and Bonwick were alluding to is that the pyramids were most likely already in existence when the Egyptian dynasties began and were built way before their arrival. It seems as if the Egyptian pharaohs were mesmerized by the monuments and built their culture around their symbology rather than the other way around. The only piece of evidence that the Great Pyramid was built by Khufu is an inscription found deep within the pyramid, which reads his name in a dubious script reminiscent of a much later writing style that was not yet developed in Khufu's time. This inscription was found in the mid-nineteenth century by the eager Richard Howard Vyse. Sitchin chronicles Vyse's adventure and ambitious drive. After Vyse was denied a partnership with professional archeologist Giovanni Caviglia, he set out on a relentless journey to gain access to the ancient sites. On February 12, 1987, during the night Vyse and a colleague snuck into the Great Pyramid and found that there was a hidden chamber. Only being

able to see it through a small hole, it would take them
months before they were able to break through the stone
slabs and find what lay behind it. What they found was a
cartouche, a royal insignia of a pharaoh. Written with
measly red paint, instead of being carved, the cartouche
read:

"Kh-u-f-u"

Leading German Egyptologist at the time, Carl Richard
Lepsius, admitted that the inscriptions "were traced with
a red brush in a cursive manner, so much so that they
resemble hieratic signs …" Lepsius among other
professional Egyptologists was concluding similar analysis
of the cartouche. The writing style matched closer with
later Egyptian writing and not that of Khufu's time. Like
others, Sitchin concluded that the Khufu inscription was

a forgery made by Vyse. This opinion is not accepted in mainstream academia, whereas astute Egyptologists firmly claim that it is a genuine inscription. The royal insignia is dubious at best and an outright forgery at worst. The British Museum's expert of hieroglyphics at that time, Samuel Birch, as Sitchin relates, said of the matter:

"Although not very legible, owing to their writing having been written in semi-hieratic or linear-hieroglyphic characters, they possess points of considerable interest."

Apart from the Khufu cartouche there were other writings, one including another royal name. This was perplexing because it would seem as if the two kings were cooperators in building the pyramid. Gaston Maspero, famed Egyptologist who discovered the Pyramid Texts, said of the unusual incident of their being two names:

"The existence of the two cartouches ... on the same monuments has caused much embarrassment on Egyptologist ..."

Sitchin concluded that the reason there were two names is that Vyse was unsure about what name to paint so he went ahead with two, to better his chances of a believable inscription. All we can conclude for sure is that the name of Khufu strangely appears in a graffiti-like manner in a blocked chamber, in the middle of the pyramid, that had to be broken into after destroying and tunneling through it. The cartouche rest in what is known as Campbell's Chamber, a cramped space belonging to the "Relieving Chambers," a chimney-like structure within the heart of the pyramid. This ambiguous structure has five spaces separated by massive stone blocks. Other than Khufu's odd cartouche, there are no other writings boasting anything about the pyramids themselves from within. The only other piece of evidence we have that gives veracity to the mainstream theory that the pyramids were built for Khufu during the fourth dynasty is a fascinating text known as Merer's logbook. The piece of papyri was found by French Egyptologist Pierre Tallet in 2013. Being found among some of the oldest surviving written records of ancient Egypt, Merer's logbook is an account of an esteemed foreman who seemingly worked for the royal court. Merer details about thirty days of differing transactions to and from Tura, Egypt's center for limestone rock. The Great Pyramids are made of mostly granite, basalt, and limestone. The Great Pyramid used to be entirely encased in a smooth white limestone finish, much different than its weathered sand look of today. Merer does make mention of gathering stone from Tura specifically to take back to the "Akhet-Khufu," which scholars agree refers to the Great Pyramid of Khufu. As exciting as the find of Merer's logbook was, there is no definitive mention of the Great Pyramid being constructed by or for Khufu or that the stones that Merer was transporting were for the construction of the pyramid. The stones he brought to the Giza Plateau could have been for anything, including the casing stones on the exterior of the pyramid. Just because the pyramid is referred to as "Akhet-Khufu" or Khufu's Pyramid doesn't necessarily mean that it was built by him and for him. It's an amazing text with immense implications for Egyptology but is still a far cry from a conclusive answer to the pyramid's construction and purpose. Tallet himself is not quick to declare this as proof that the pyramids were built by our distant Egyptian relatives saying to *Smithsonian Magazine* in 2015:

"I really don't want to be involved in any polemics on the building of the pyramids at Giza—it's not my job ... Of course it's interesting to have this kind of information, it will deserve a lot of study."

The last piece of information regarding the pyramids I'll briefly investigate is the famous Inventory Stele of Khufu. This text has troubled mainstream academics because of its contradictory statements about the dating of the Sphinx. Discovered by Auguste Marriete in 1858, this tablet was written by an unknown scribe in the seventh century BCE. The text centers around a "Temple of Isis," which does exist in the Giza Plateau and goes all the way back to Khufu's time. This temple had been

rebuilt and renamed over the millennia, not known as the

Temple of Isis in Khufu's time. What makes this stele

intriguing is that the scribe boasts that Khufu, upon

finding the ancient temple, rebuilt it, and also restored or

repaired the Sphinx. Reading from famed alternative

historian and American associate professor of Natural

Sciences at the College of General Studies of Boston

University Robert M. Shoch's "The Inventory Stele:

More Fact than Fiction," we find that Khufu made some

minor repair to the Sphinx's backside and sought to make

plans for other needed restoration. Shoch, referencing the

1906 translation by James Henry Breasted of the stele,

presents that the Sphinx is clearly shown in hieroglyphic

form and referred to as "Hor-Em-Akhet," the "Guardian

of the Atmosphere," and that it was "lacking guilded

stone …" This is fascinating because it completely undermines the mainstream idea that the Sphinx was built after Khufu by his son, Khafre. Now what is also interesting is that the Inventory Stele claims that Khufu built two pyramids, one for himself and one for his wife. Interestingly, a later 1991 translation by French Egyptologist Christiane Zivie-Coche, fixes the translation as Khufu, "rebuilding" or "restoring" these pyramids. Zivie-Coche states in *Sphinx: History of a Monument*:

"The consecration text on the stela evokes what were undoubtedly renovations, not new constructions: renovations of the pyramids of Cheops and the royal daughter Henutsen, and of the temple of Isis itself."

Although this text is seen as a fanatical work to justify the later Egyptian cult of Isis, it again throws more ambiguity into the matter. If the Sphinx was already constructed before Khufu, then we can assume that so were the pyramids. All we can do is speculate from what we have. What we have available to us is some sketchy graffiti bearing Khufu's name in a later writing style within an awkward part of the Great Pyramid, Merer's logbook, accounting for limestone blocks beings taken to the Giza Plateau during the reign of Khufu, and the Inventory Stele, written thousands of years later, claiming that Khufu seemingly resorted the Sphinx and Great Pyramid.

I decided to go over this enigma because the pyramids are a paragon for the mystery of the ancient esoteric past. After all the years passed and evidence gained, we still cannot uniformly conclude why or by who they were built. I'd like to go over a few interesting alternative points about the Great Pyramids before continuing on to what else of the Anunnaki may remain.

The Great Pyramid weighs over thirteen billion pounds, containing 2.3 million individual blocks of stone. One block would have to be laid every five minutes, every hour, twenty-four hours a day, for twenty years or so in order to logistically achieve the building of the pyramid in the time frame we are told it was built in. Its enigmatic ambiguity hides its original purpose; however, its mathematical properties give away some clues. In 1983, independent Egyptologist and author Robert Bauval revealed an interesting feature about the three pyramids of Giza. He noticed that the smaller pyramid of Mankaure was slightly offset from the other two. Later on, he would claim in his 1994 book, *The Orion Mystery: Unlocking the Secrets of the Pyramids*, that the three pyramids are a representation of the three stars of Orion's Belt, which also have an off-kilter star. He stated:

"The correlation was stunning. Not only did the layout of the pyramids match the stars with uncanny precision but the intensity of the stars, shown by their apparent size, corresponded with the Giza group."

Following his intuition, Bauval used a computer program to simulate when the constellation of Orion would have linked directly over the Great Pyramids in the night sky. He found that they once connected together around 10,500 BCE. This is a fascinating number, going back about eight thousand years further than the accepted build date of the Great Pyramids. What's also fascinating is that at this time, in the Age of Leo, the constellation of the lion faced directly in front of the Great Sphinx. It seems as though the original builders were commemorating the construction with the age of Leo, also stamping the image of the Sphinx as a remembrance of when they were built. Bauval also noted that the Sphinx and pyramids, representing their celestial counterparts also rested by the Nile river, which was to represent the Milky Way Galaxy. The Egyptians placed importance on celestial matters. As Bauval and others have noted, the Egyptians built their sacred structures on sites that would mirror the celestial structures above. They believed in preparing themselves for an afterlife of ascending to the Duat or place of the dead, where they would await judgment by their beloved gods. This journey was to be taken through the heavens above, by their soul. By mirroring the heavens above down below, the Egyptians could be in direct connection with the source of all.

In an esoteric text known as the *Tabula Smaragdina* or *Emerald Tablet*, we find the great alchemical axiom, "As Above So Below." The *Emerald Tablet*, although having uncertain origins, some speculating a Greek origin, represents itself as having knowledge passed down from the ancient wisdom god of Egypt, Thoth. This axiom presents a divine concept that states mankind on earth is inseparable from God up above. As the Bible states, we are made from the image of God; thus, all things on earth are a microcosm of a larger organization. It is a concept of micro and macrocosms being inextricably connected through the mechanism of destiny. The *Tabula Smaragdina* belongs to the line of "Hermetic texts," named after the Greek rendition of the god Thoth. A later famous addition to the *Emerald Tablet* is the twentieth-century book *Emerald Tablets of Thoth the Atlantean.* It was published by American mystic, author, and founder of the Brotherhood of the White Temple, Dr. M Doreal. Doreal claimed he was given permission to translate the Emerald Tablets inscribed by the god Thoth by Tibetan monks in the Himalayas. In Doreal's work we find that it was the god Thoth who had built the Great Pyramid as a regeneration chamber. Thoth, in the tablets, speaks about the "Halls of Amenti" deep within the pyramid in which his body rests in a cryogenic-type state, while his consciousness roams freely. The pyramid, according to the text, was built as an initiation temple into the mysteries of life and death. It was constructed with metaphysical properties that would allow the adepts to harness energetic powers to ascend this reality or regenerate one's soul, freeing it from the cycle of death. As Thoth boasts in this passage:

"Free was I of the Halls of Amenti, bound not by death to the circle of life. Far to the stars I journeyed until space and time became as naught."

The location of the Great Pyramid was chosen with purpose. Dr. Joseph Seiss, author and theologian, demonstrated in 1877 that the Great Pyramid of Giza is located at the exact center of the "land mass" of the earth, basically at the center of the world. The Great Pyramid can also be used as a compass with its sides pointing to the true north, south, east and west axes. Seiss wonderfully defends the Great Pyramid in the following quote:

"It has been ascertained and clearly demonstrated that there is in the measures, pointings, form, and features of that great primeval monument … a massive and indestructible stone memorial of a complete and faultless knowledge of the structure of the universe, of the exact and physical sciences both terrestrial and cosmical, a determination of a perfect system of weights and measures scientifically conformed to what the Opifex Mundi (Creator of the World) fixed in things when he fetched a compass round the worlds and weighed the hills in balances. Scientific investigation on the part of different men competent to the task have made it clear that there is built into that edifice a record of the heavens at the time of its erection which gives its age by astronomy in full accord with all external indications and evidences; also a record of the size, form and weight of the earth and its relation to and distance from the sun, the true length of the solar year, the number of years in the precessional cycle, the average temperature of the habitable world, together with the multitudinous cosmical facts and mathematical formulas and proportions no better told by sciences now existing among men" (Joseph Seiss, Gospel in the Stars, p. 175).

Seiss was referring to the esoteric attributes of the Great Pyramid that have been claimed by alternative scholars. The Great Pyramid has mathematical numbers built into it that can be used to decipher other aspects of nature or more so, remember those aspects of nature. For example, any given side of the Great Pyramid is about 365 cubits long, the exact number of days in a general year. Many scholars have pointed out that the Great Pyramid is a mathematical scale model of the earth. Specifically, a 1:43,200 scale. Quoting Hancock in *Fingerprints of the Gods* we find that: "Earth's equatorial circumference, 24,902.4.5 miles" when divided or scaled down by 43,200, "we get 0.5764ths of a mile." When we convert this to feet we get the surprising perimeter of the Great Pyramid, 3,043.39, give or take several feet. The fact that the pyramid is a scale model of the earth's circumference by 1:43,200 is intriguing. The number 432 is found, just like pi and the Fibonacci sequence, throughout sacred instances. Quoting from computer science and math major Hans Sebastian:

"In Hindu cosmology, a Yuga Cycle lasts 4320000 years, the time from Adam to Noah up until the flood was 86400 weeks. Half of 86400 is 43200. Noah was 600 years old when the flood came, and 600 X 72 is 43200. 72 is the number of hidden names of God in Judaism and were used by Moses to part the Red Sea. The number of years it takes the Earth to complete 1 degree of its precession is 72. As above, 72 X 600 = 43200. Babylonia was ruled by ten kings for 432000 years before the flood came. On the Day of Ragnarok, which is the battle at the end of days in Norse Mythology, it is said that 800 warriors will come out of each of 540 doors to fight alongside Odin. 800 X 540 = 43200."

432 Hz is also seen as a healing frequency that has been used in ancient times by New Age adherents. The Great Pyramid engineers also utilized the irrational transcendental number of pi to design its miraculous qualities. Quoting from an article on LiveScience.com from Pulitzer Prize-winner, writer and physicist Natalie Wolchover, we see that pi:

"Crops up in the natural world, too. It appears everywhere there's a circle, of course, such as the disk of the sun, the spiral of the DNA double helix, the pupil of the eye, the concentric rings that travel outward from splashes in ponds. Pi also appears in the physics that describes waves, such as ripples of light and sound. It even enters into the equation that defines how precisely we can know the state of the universe, known as Heisenberg's uncertainty principle."

Now I'll admit, I'm no mathematician so I'm basically quoting various sources on the following math about how the Great Pyramid utilized pi to encode a useful measuring tool that could give us information about our own planet and celestial matters. Seventy-eight-year-old Egyptologist at the time John Taylor, wrote in his 1850s *The Great Pyramid: Why Was It Built and Who Built It?* about the designers of the pyramid that:

"They assumed the earth to be a perfect sphere … and as they knew that the radius of a circle must bear a certain proportion to its circumference, they then built a Pyramid of such a height in proportion to its base, that its perpendicular would be equal to the radius of a circle equal in circumference to the perimeter of the base."

Taylor was much ahead of his time in realizing this fact. Taylor was convinced that the pyramid was not built by ancient Egyptians but by foreigners to the land who were instructed to build it with divine purpose with divine units of measure by God. The mathematical divine number of pi is built into the Great Pyramid as explained by Graham Hancock in his famed *Fingerprints of the Gods*. He details in a section titled "Eternal Numbers" that the ratio between the Great Pyramid's height, and the perimeter of its base, is the same as "the ratio between the radius and the circumference of a circle, i.e., 2pi …" Basically stating that its measurements were calculated by using similar mechanics of pi. This feature of the pyramid is a grand mathematical achievement known as "squaring the circle." Again, not something I totally understand but I will still relay for those who can or seek to. Nineteenth-century British author and contemporary of Taylor wrote:

"The chief objects of these buildings [is] to serve for sepulchral monuments, the Egyptians sought, in the appropriate figure of the Pyramid, to perpetuate, at the same time, a portion of their geometrical science."

Agnew realized that the science behind the design of the Great Pyramids was achieving the almost impossible of squaring the circle. A basic Wikipedia explanation of this obstacle is as follows:

"Squaring the circle is a problem in geometry first proposed in Greek mathematics. It is the challenge of constructing a square with the area of a circle by using only a finite number of steps with compass and straightedge. The difficulty of the problem raised the question of whether specified axioms of Euclidean geometry concerning the existence of lines and circles implied the existence of such a square."

The "squaring of a circle" basically means creating a square and circle with the same perimeter or area. This mathematical puzzle or equation has been attempted for thousands of years by many great minds including the introspective Greek philosophers. Plutarch wrote in his *On Exile* that Anaxagoras was the first to try and solve the issue stating:

"There is no place that can take away the happiness of a man, nor yet his virtue or wisdom. Anaxagoras, indeed, wrote on the squaring of the circle while in prison."

This seemingly impossible feat of creating a basic square and circle with equal perimeters was ideologically achieved within the alignments of the Great Pyramid. If you take the height of the Great Pyramid to be a radius of a circumference of a circle, that circle's area would be the exact perimeter of the square base of the Great

Pyramid, (see figure 1).

Figure 1

*Height of Great Pyramid equals a radius of a circumference of a circle

that would perfectly encapsulate the pyramid within a circle.

Thus, the Great Pyramid was a testament to that which is impossible. The importance of this was seemingly less about math and more about spiritual matters. As explained by author Robert Lawlor in his book *Sacred Geometry Philosophy and Practice*:

"Because the circle is an incommensurable figure based on π, it is impossible to draw a square more than approximately equal to it. Nevertheless, the Squaring of the Circle is of great importance to the geometer-cosmologist because for him the circle represents pure, un-manifest spirit-space, while the square represents the manifest and comprehensible world. When a near-equality is drawn between the circle and square, the infinite is able to express its dimensions or qualities through the finite."

Squaring the circle in esoteric means would be to adjoin Heaven and earth, creating an energetic force that embodies the great axiom "As above, so below." The

Great Pyramid used to be totally encased in white polished limestone, which could intensely reflect light; its shine could be seen from space as a star on earth. The placements of the Great Pyramids, as noted by Bauval, are interesting. They were seated with sacredness in mind. The very word *pyramid* is said to have derived from the Greek *pyramidos* or "fire in the middle." The Greeks may have utilized the Semitic word *urrim-midden*, "light-measures," for their translation. The actual ancient Egyptian word for pyramid was *khuti*, glorious light. The pyramids of Egypt might have also been placed where they are according to the science of ley lines. Famed author, researcher, esotericist, and creator of various New Age schools Drunvalo Melchezidek, has said of Thoth and the pyramid:

"According to Thoth, because of the placement of the Great Pyramid on the Earth connecting into the Earth's huge geometrical field—specifically the octahedral field of the Earth, which is equivalent to our own fields—and because of the pyramid's mass and the geometries used in it, the white-light energy field spirals upward and becomes extremely strong, stretching all the way out to the center of the galaxy. The dark-light energy comes in from above, spirals through zero point and connects with the center of the Earth. In this way the Great Pyramid connects the center of the Earth to the center of our galaxy."—Drunvalo Melchizedek, The Ancient Secret of the Flower of Life: Volume 2

There are definitely mathematical and geographical anomalies built into the Great Pyramid and when taken into metaphysical consideration, the implications of these parameters could create amazing scientific potentiality for quantum functions as stated by Drunvalo. Amateur archeologist Alfred Watkins was the first among modern times to realize that many ancient sacred sites were all positioned in areas that could be connected with precise lines on a map. Watkins called these "ley lines." Before him, William Black gave a talk to the British Archeological Association in 1870 titled "Boundaries and Landmarks." In this talk he revealed that "Monuments exist marking grand geometrical lines which cover the whole of Western Europe." It has been noted by many scholars since then that there is some eerie alignment with certain sacred sites across whole countries to other sacred sites. In his famous book *The Old Straight Track*, Watkins theorized that these ley lines were initially set up as guiding posts to be used as useful highways in the days without digital navigation. He also theorized that some of the ley lines were constructed as acts of religious veneration stating:

"It has become plain that the topographical sites used for sun alignment and those for the ley are in some cases identical, and that the alignment is often the same for both uses."

For example, there is the famous "Saint Michael's line" that runs through Britain, hitting important churches and archaic sites. John Michell, in his 1969 *The View Over Atlantis*, says of Saint Michael's line:

"[It] is remarkable for its length and accuracy. It appears to be set between two prominent Somerset hills, both dedicated to St. Michael with ruined churches on their summit. These two hills are Glastonbury Tor and 'The Mump' at Burrowbridge some ten miles to the south-west. Both these hills appear to have been artificially shaped so that their axis align with each other ..."

German contemporary of Watkins Wilhelm Teudt advanced this theory in his *Germanic Sanctuaries*. He found that in Germany too, there were archaic sites that seemingly lined up for some sort of ancient religious reason. He called these "Helige Linien" (Holy-Lines).

Many within the New Age community have extrapolated the theory, claiming that ley lines were implemented to give certain structures an energetic boost by placing them in areas with heightened connections to earth's magnetic sphere or such. One thing is for sure, the alignments do exist and can be traversed as efficient travel guides from one end of a land mass to another. I point this out to say, whoever was building these ancient sites like the Great Pyramids of Egypt, was doing so for purposes we have yet to fully understand. We are far removed from these great builders because they are gone. Interestingly enough the oldest known written records so far have been found in Sumer. They were uncovered in the twentieth century at the library of the ancient city of Nippur. One of these records is the "Kesh temple hymn." Written in 2600 BCE, the Kesh temple hymn is a veneration of the gods. Specifically, the hymn is praising the gods for building several structures (houses as they are titled) that seemingly hold great importance. The "houses" are all part of a major structure known as the Kec. As the inscription reads:

"Enlil, the princely one, came forth from the house ... House Kec, platform of the Land, important fierce bull! Growing as high as the hills, embracing the heavens ... House founded by An, praised by Enlil, given an oracle by mother Nintud! House Kec, green in its fruit! Will anyone else bring forth something as great as Kec? ... House of the Anuna gods possessing great power, which gives wisdom to the people; house, reposeful dwelling of the great gods!"

To think that the oldest surviving written record known to our entire existence as a human race is this text, the Kesh temple hymn, praising the gods for building an awe-inspiring building that reaches the heavens, is at the very least strange. Another interesting aspect of this structure mentioned in the text is the fact that at its gate is a great sphinxlike monument, as it attests:

"House in whose interior is the power of the Land, and behind which is the life of Sumer at whose gate is a lion reclining on its paws, at whose gate is the ruler who decides cases! House at whose door is the Great Mountain without adversary ..."

I won't be fanatic enough to claim that this is proof the Anunnaki built the pyramids and the sphinx of Giza; however, again, to think that this, the oldest text of our human lineage, is praising the building of an important temple dedicated to the gods is astounding. The text is at least as old as 2600 BCE. The historical events must be older; how much older we don't know. In the text are clear indications of a priesthood dating back at least to this era if not older as is stated:

"The house whose lords are the Anuna gods, whose nuec priests are the sacrificers of en priest [...] holds the lead-rope dangling. The a-tu priests holds the staff; the [...] brings the [...] waters. The [...] takes his seat in the holy place; the enkum priests bow down [...]. The pacec priests beat the drumskins; they recite powerfully, powerfully. The bull's horn is made to growl; the drumsticks are made to thud. The singer cries out to the ala drum; the grand sweet tigi is played for him. The house is built; its nobility is good! The house Kec is built; its nobility is good! Its lady has taken a seat in its [...]. Ninhursaja, its lady, has taken her seat in its [...]. Will anyone else bring forth something as great as Kec?"

It is obvious here that our ancestors partook in ritual ceremonies worshipping the Anunnaki and their accomplishments. The art and sacredness of building temples were important to the past. The religious rites may still be practiced, the temples may still stand but the gods are gone.

Among the fascinating Hermetic texts is the "Asclepius" text. Also known as *The Perfect Discourse,* this text presents a sobering prophecy by Thoth, the supposed builder of the Great Pyramid in the Emerald Tablets of Thoth the Atlantean, to Asclepius, a disciple of his at the time. It is a legendary tale, taking place thousands of years ago when the God Thoth was still among us. The actual text is dated to a now lost Greek original thought to be from at least the second to third centuries CE. Although the text itself doesn't refer to Thoth, it was believed in Hellenistic times that the Greek Hermes was a rendition of the Egyptian Thoth. Both cultures saw similarities during their cultural mixing between these two gods. From that renaissance arose an anachronistic archetype known as Hermes-Trismegistus, an amalgamation of Thoth and Hermes. This sage was purported to have crafted sacred teachings that he left behind in copied lessons known generally as the *Corpus Hermeticum*. The collection mostly consists of Greek writings from the early Christian era, with Egyptian symbology written into its myth. The oldest surviving manuscript of the Asclepius is a Latin translation from the fourth to fifth centuries CE. It is a great philosophical text to conclude my coverage of the Great Pyramids here and to continue on to the reason why we won't meet any Anunnaki. Quoting from

Clement Salaman's 2007 translation *Asclepius: The Perfect Discourse of Hermes Trismegistus* we find that Thoth says of Egypt:

"Egypt is the image of heaven; or to speak more precisely, all things which are set in motion and regulated in heaven have been transferred, or have descended, into Egypt? More truthfully still, our land is the temple of the whole cosmos." He goes on to prophesize saying: "The gods will withdraw from earth to heaven and Egypt will be deserted. The land which used to be the seat of religion will be abandoned by the gods and become void of their presence. Not only will foreigners, pouring into the region and covering this land, neglect religion, but what is worse, religion, duties to the gods and divine worship will be prohibited with penalties prescribed by so-called laws. This holy land, this home of sanctuaries and temples, will all be filled with sepulchres and the dead. O Egypt, Egypt, only stories of your religion will survive, and these your children will not believe. Only words carved in stone will narrate your pious deeds."

And in this we find our philosophical answer at the very least. The Anunnaki are nowhere to be found because they are gone. All that is left is the remains of unexplainable monuments and strange texts with adventurous tales of our ancestors. Not only are they gone, but they might have never existed. The tale of the gods could also just be a myth, made up to justify what we don't understand or worse, to justify kingship and population control. My intent with this work isn't to speculate whether the gods were real; they were real in the minds of our ancestors just as God is in the minds of modern people. My intent is to show that the dogmatic myths of our modern religions stem from the Sumerian stories. However, I do not doubt that the gods could have existed. There are indications of lost civilizations and definitely existing remnants of those as seen in the strange, enigmatic structures like the pyramids. The "gods" could have very well been our prehistoric ancestors who merely restarted civilization after major cataclysms, simply posing as gods. I will speculate on this further later in the book; however, for now I think it's logical to say whatever the gods were, they're not here now.

The Sumerians made an everlasting impact on the old world that would follow humanity up to modern times. Their gods were adopted by their contemporaries. It was the Sumerian gods who created us and set the foundations of civilization and life within Sumer to be prosperous, according to their scriptures. In a fascinating and lengthy tale known as "Enki and the World Order," we see that Sumer was once a place adored by the gods. It was designed, domesticated, and ordained to be special. In the text Enki is pridefully complimenting and basking in the glory that once was Sumer, the land of the gods as we see in this quote from Oxford's online lexicon translation:

"Sumer, Great Mountain, land of heaven and earth, trailing glory, bestowing powers on the people from sunrise to sunset: your powers are superior powers, untouchable, and your heart is complex and inscrutable. Like heaven itself, your good creative force ... in which gods too can be born, is beyond reach. Giving birth to kings who put on the good diadem, giving birth to lords who wear the crown on their heads—your lord, the honoured lord, sits with An the king on An's dais. Your king, the Great Mountain, father Enlil, the father of all the lands, has blocked you impenetrably like a cedar tree. The Anuna, the great gods, have taken up dwellings in your midst, and consume their food in your *giguna* shrines with their single trees. Household Sumer, may your sheepfolds be built and your cattle multiply, may your *giguna* touch the skies. May your good temples reach up to heaven. May the Anuna determine the destinies in your midst."

These majestic scenes and powerful deities are mystical memories of the past. Although the gods always remained with the people either in spirit or through mythical tales even long after the Sumerian culture, unfortunately the Sumerians themselves did eventually face a fateful end. With Sumer's decline went its admiration and connection to the Anunnaki, as they knew it, eventually leading to the monotheistic realm of the major world religions.

The beginning of civilization is hard to detail conclusively due to lost written records and archeology. What we know is that right around 3500 BCE, the Sumerian civilization arose. Its people knew themselves as the "Sag.gi.ga," (Black-Headed People). They were later called Sumerians by their rivals, the Akkadians. *Sumer* meant "land of the civilized kings," thus the Sumerians were the people of the land of kings. Rightfully so, Sumer was the first civilized society that formulated laws, governance, and social structures. However, the Sumerians didn't pop up out of nowhere; they formulated themselves out of the many nomadic tribes that existed within Arabia. Although the Sumerian culture would go on to influence the pre-Judaic and Judeo-Christian world, the Sumerians weren't actually Semitic people. Although they wrote in cuneiform as did the following kingdoms, they spoke an entirely different type of dialect, not akin to the Semitic languages that would lead up to Hebrew. Cuneiform is a style of writing, a font per se, not a language.

The early Sumerians were a democratic people, settling matters on a local level, electing officials only for agricultural developments and day-to-day operations. Once their individual city-states started to fully develop, there suddenly became a reason for a diplomatic ruler within each city. Each city had a patron deity that was a symbolic overseer of the city. Underneath the god there would be the En (priest), accompanied by the Ensi (governor), and the Lugal, a sort of military or kingly ruler. Sumer was situated in what is now known as Iraq, in the Middle East or Mesopotamia, meaning "Land between the Two Rivers" titled so by the Greeks. During Sumer's prime there were twelve city-states, starting with

Kish. Sumer's entire history surrounds a struggle for central power; no one person was able to unify all of Sumer long enough to sustain itself against the evolving world around it. Many tried, such as Lugal-anne-mundu, who, according to a seventeenth-century BCE inscription, boasted of having subjugated several rival cities outside of Sumer. Ruling in the twenty-fifth century BCE, part of his later inscribed military exploit quotes him as saying:

"For Nintu, the mother of the nation, queen for the temple, great spouse of Enlil, his beloved lady I, Lugalanamundu, the strong man, who provides for Nippur, king of Adab and king of the four world quarters secured tribute upon the people of all the lands ..."

We see here Lugal-anne-mundu following a necessary protocol of calling upon the Anunnaki as justification for

his conquest, a claim many after him would repeat.
Mundu ruled for about ninety years over the various city-states of Sumer but after his death Sumer fell right back into warring states and chaos. There were bitter rivalries between many sister cities. One king would rise from a certain city, attempt to overtake the other, meet an untimely death or defeat in battle then another king from a different city would repeat the same fate. For example, the cities of Umma and Lagash faced intense battles with each other for Sumerian supremacy. King of Lagash, Eannatum 2450 BCE, was a fierce leader who did overtake many major cities within Sumer including Umma. After being killed in battle, the throne was up for grabs again. The last of the old dynastic time period to rise to the throne would be Lugalzaggesi, from Umma. He destroyed Lagash, burning and looting it to the

ground. Surprisingly one of the surviving texts from Lagash after the destruction was a legal document expressing the individual freedoms that the citizens were privileged to, showcasing just how intellectual the Sumerians could be. An inscription boasting the efforts of Lugalzaggesi stated that he ruled "from the Lower Sea [Persian Gulf] to the Upper Sea [Mediterranean]." However, as the Sumerians battled among each other, outside of Sumer in the wider world of Arabia and the Far East, the other nomadic tribes festered into full-fledged organized societies as well. Upon Lugalzaggesi's Sumer descended the neighboring Akkadians. Led by the famous Sargon of Akkad, Sumer was brutally defeated. Strangely we don't know Sargon's real name, origin of birth or how he was able to swiftly rise to power. As pioneering Assyriologist Samuel Noah Kramer details in his *Cradle of Civilization*, Sargon's birth was mythical. Sargon is a title he gave to himself, meaning "legitimate ruler." Not much is known of him but according to his alleged autobiography known as *The Legend of Sargon*, his mother was a priestess who belonged to the temple of Inanna. This tale was published by Sir Henry Rawlinson in 1870, after its discovery at the Library of Ashurbanipal in Nineveh. Sargon, according to the tale, never knew his father, which alludes to a divine birth. Being a priestess, loyal to the disciplinary regulations, his mother birthed him then carefully placed him in a basket and floated him down the Euphrates river. He was later found by a gardener who worked for the king of Kish. Sargon, explaining his humble beginnings in the tale, appealed to the ordinary working class. Scholars see this appeal as a ploy to distance himself from the previous Sumerian rulers who all claimed divine rule. Although he doesn't entirely sway from the divine right to rule claim. Sargon mentions that as he grew up alongside Akki the gardener, it was Inanna that favored him and "granted him her love." It's unclear what this means but we can assume this meant she adorned him to be ruler? As Sumer was facing problems unifying under Lugalzaggesi south in Umma, Sargon, ethnically an Akkadian, eventually seized the opportunity to surprise and dismantle the disheveled kingdom of Sumer. Historian Susan Wise Bauer writes on this, saying:

"Sargon's relatively speedy conquest of the entire Mesopotamian plain is startling ..." The Sumerians "were suffering from an increased gap between elite leadership and poor laborers. [The rich] used their combined religious and secular power to claim as much as three-quarters of the land in any given city for themselves.

Sargon's relatively easy conquest of the area (not to mention his constant carping on his own non-aristocratic background) may reveal a successful appeal to the downtrodden members of Sumerian society to come over to his side."

Sargon ruled far and wide, demolishing any real chance of the Sumerian Empire to rise in full again. The Sumerian language began to fade out, as it became customary for Akkadian to be the state language and writing norm. He ruled fiercely for about fifty years until his death, which again caused a disorganized kingdom followed by his two sons. It wasn't until his grandson Naram-Sin arose to the throne that Akkad would resume power, quelling the rising Sumerian rebellions. After about another fifty years in 2200 BCE, Akkad and Sumer were ravished by another nomadic group of peoples known as the Gutians. They were aggressive barbarians that leveled the kingdom's capital at Agade. Sumer and Mesopotamia fell into another broken period. In an Old Babylonian text known as the "Curse of Agade," we see just how distraught the Sumerian people were by this invasion:

"Enlil brought out of the mountains those who do not resemble other people, who are not reckoned as part of the Land, the Gutians, an unbridled people, with human intelligence but canine instincts and monkeys' features. Like small birds they swooped on the ground in great flocks. Because of Enlil, they stretched their arms out across the plain like a net for animals. Nothing escaped their clutches, no one left their grasp."—Oxford ETCSL

The epic places the horrible event as revenge by the god Enlil on the land for the destruction of the holy temples by Naram-Sin. Out of this time arose Utuhegal from Erech, a mighty and proud ruler. He drove out the

Gutians and restored Sumer. From Utuhegal Sumer flourished into its final dynastic period known as the Neo-Sumerian era. Of course, his reign was predictably short, in Sumerian fashion. After seven years, he was deposed by Ur-Nammu. Sumer regained some of its glory, reinstating its language, customs, and infrastructure, enjoying a last period of Sumerian identity. Around 1750 BCE the Sumerian civilization officially ended with more outside invasion, starting with the Elamites, and ending with the Amorite kings who would usher in the kingdom of Babylon.

Sumer's beautiful intelligence as the world's first civilization crumbled to virtual extinction. The Black-Headed People left behind what are known as "Lamentation Texts," which spoke of the drastic decline.

Among the domestic rivalries and wars with outsiders, there were also natural causes that added to the chaos. Matt Konfirst, a geologist at the Byrd Polar Research Center, presented some geological evidence for what might have been a two-hundred- to three-hundred-year drought that flashed over the land unfortunately right at the onset of the Gutian invasion. This drought was spoken of within the *Curse of Agade* text wailing that:

"The large arable tracts yielded no grain, the inundated fields yielded no fish, the irrigated orchards yielded no syrup or wine, the thick clouds did not rain."

In what is known as the *Lamentation of UR,* written around the invasion of the Elamites in 2000 BCE, the Sumerians talk about an "evil wind" that swept over the land causing a regression of life. As is seen here in this Oxford translation:

"The storm that annihilates the Land roars below—the people groan. The evil wind, like a rushing torrent, cannot be restrained …"

The text goes on to speak about a devastating scene where Sumer is destroyed in flames, buildings are toppled, and bodies are lying around everywhere:

"Like a flood storm it completely destroyed the city. The storm that annihilates the Land silenced the city. The storm that will make anything vanish came doing evil … On its boulevards where festivals had been held, heads lay scattered. In all its streets where walks had been taken, corpses were piled. In its places where the dances of the Land had taken place, people were stacked in heaps. They made the blood of the Land flow down the wadis like copper or tin. Its corpses, like fat left in the sun, melted away of themselves …"

The Sumerian civilization gave us so much that we take for granted these days; from them sprang the modern world. More importantly to this book, the greatest impression the Sumerians gave to the evolving world after them was the worship of the gods. After their fall new empires would rise, most notably Babylon, which would be among the last carrying the torch of the old world with loyalties to the Anunnaki. It would be Babylon's battle with the Kingdom of Judah that would eventually lead to the overthrow of the old world and the birth of a new era, the age of monotheism, the age of the gods forgotten.

"Lugalzagesi, king of Uruk, king of the nation,

incantation-priest of An … looked upon truly

by An as the king of all the lands. The chief ruler of Enlil,

given wisdom by Enki … chief steward of the gods."

This royal decree was given by the aforementioned king of Sumer before the Akkadian invasion, Lugalzagesi. Being remembered as the first true king of a unified Sumer during its old kingdom period, Lugalzagesi ruled about three hundred years after the Kesh temple hymn was written. The gods if not corporally real, were definitely held in spirit for hundreds if not thousands of years. At the top of the family tree were Anu and his wives Antu and Ki. Below them were the famous brother gods Enki and Enlil; from them sprang the many grandchildren and great-grandchildren of Anu who would also hold important titles and host famous epics of their own within ancient Mesopotamian tales. It was the worship of these varying gods that would cause battles, discrepancies, and wars among the city-states of ancient Mesopotamia. When Sargon overtook Sumer, he instituted his daughter Enheduanna as the high priestess of Sumer's most important temple in the city of Ur. She left behind a few texts of her own, which exalt the goddess Inanna, later known as Ishtar in the classical world. As is seen in her text known as *The exaltation of Inana:*

"I, En-hedu-ana, will recite a prayer to you. To you, holy Inana, … Most precious lady, beloved by An, your holy heart is great; may it be assuaged on my behalf! … you are the great lady of the horizon and zenith of the heavens. The Anuna have submitted to you. From birth you were the junior queen: how supreme you are now over the Anuna, the great gods! The Anuna kiss the ground with their lips before you."

Inanna is remembered throughout Mesopotamian history as the fierce, warlike great-granddaughter of Anu. She was worshiped and loved by the Akkadians as well as other kingdoms. The last kingdom to remain aggressively loyal to the Anunnaki was Babylon. In the Bible, Babylon is the mortal enemy to the kingdom of Judah because of the havoc the Babylonians wrought onto the peoples especially during the destruction of the temple and enslaving of the people during the Babylonian captivity. The last ruler of Babylon was a king named Nabonidus. This ruler also left behind decrees that mentioned the Anunnaki. Translated by Paul-Alain Beaulieu, author of *The Reign of Nabonidus*, King of Babylon 556–539 BCE

(1989), we see in the Nabonidus Cylinder Seal, Nabonidus declare:

"In the beginning of my everlasting reign, they sent me a dream. Marduk, the great lord, and Sin, the luminary of heaven and the netherworld, stood together. Marduk spoke with me: 'Nabonidus, king of Babylon, carry bricks on your riding horse, rebuild Ehulhul and cause Sin, the great lord, to establish his residence in its midst.'"

Here Nabonidus declares that he saw the gods Marduk and Sin, two grandchildren of the Sumerian god Anu, in a dream. In this vision the gods told him to rebuild an important ancient temple known as the Elhulhul. Nabonidus ruled from 539–536 BCE. This is about two thousand years after the Kesh temple hymn, the oldest script mentioning the gods. What is interesting is that unlike the older text Nabonidus mentions that he saw the gods in a vision, giving him the right to rule and restore an ancient temple. Also, Nabonidus praises Marduk, a younger god not primarily worshipped until after Sumer. Marduk is the son of Enki and the nephew of Enlil. However, Nabonidus does mention Enlil as a title for Marduk saying:

"Reverently, I spoke to the Enlil of the gods, Marduk: 'That temple which you ordered me to build, the Mede surrounds it and his might is excessive.' But Marduk spoke with me: 'The Mede whom you mentioned, he, his country and the kings who march at his side will be no more.'"

Enlil means Lord of the Wind in Sumerian. Enlil was a central god in the holy triad of the Sumerian pantheon consisting of Anu, Enki and Enlil. So, in this reference to Marduk being an "Enill of the Gods," Nabonidus is venerating Marduk in a highly respectful fashion. At this time, it seems that the older gods are not present in the same corporeal sense let alone the younger gods either, for they visited Nabonidus in a dream. It is at this point where the gods become to fade into a more spiritual concept rather than great personages who once walked among the people, creating buildings, and instituting the basic forms of civilized life. In another peculiar text during this time, we see that in fact the god Sin, also known as Nanna, left earth. In the Adad-Guppi Stele, Nabonidus's mother wails to the lunar deity of Harran, Sin, to return to the forsaken city, crying out:

"I am Adad-guppi, the mother of Nabonidus. Sin left Harran, but I kept worshiping, praying, managing a humble life, and offering gifts … Sin, king of gods, help my son, Nabonidus, not to commit sin and protect him by sending helping angels …"

Here at the end of the Babylonian Empire right before the onset of what would become the formation of Judaism and the Old Testament, we see remnants of the Anunnaki reduced to distant gods, who have left earth, only available through visions. Adad-Guppi the mother of Nabonidus pleas to Sin in her inscription to send "helping angels." This shows how our ancient ancestors viewed the Anunna at this point: They were ethereal distant beings. History, at least Judeo-Christian history, up until modern times is basically the story of warring kingdoms fighting over sacred lands in the Middle East, declaring divine right to do so by their patron Anunnaki god. As time went on the need for this justification changed from the gods commissioning the conquest to complex political altruisms causing us to invade countries. The idea of fighting for our country under

God's favor, however, is still present. It seems as if our human need to serve for God, rooted in our worship of the Anunnaki, still reverberates through our habits.

Chapter 4

The Cover-Up

Society is shaped by popular ideas. The way we view ourselves and the way we perceive history is influenced by ideas that take hold in the minds of the masses. Our modern world for the last two thousand years for the most part has revolved around the Judeo-Christian and Islamic standpoint. It wasn't until relatively recently within the grand scope of our entire history that liberal ideals began to sway the masses from the fetters of a religiously run world. And with this process of collective perception comes the abrupt intervening of totalitarian rule, which at times deliberately destroys peoples, archeology and documents that once held influence on our world. With this destruction comes a forcing of ideals, an unnatural process that indoctrinates society instead of allowing it to think for itself. The change from polytheistic belief to a monotheistic one in our major religious institutions occurred over a slow-burning process that underwent the two aforementioned changes. As the days of the ancient past moved on, the way we viewed the deities of old shifted and in some cases the history of them was deliberately covered up.

In a video presented by Arabian channel MEMRI TV, in 2016, titled "Iraqi Transport Minister Kazem Finjan: 5,000-Year-Old Sumerian Airport Served for Space Travel," Iraqi transport minister Finjan passionately exclaims that his Mesopotamian ancestors, the Sumerians, built the world's first airport. He wildly claimed that the Sumerians used the vast desert plateau of the Middle East as an efficient landing corridor to take off to distant planets. It's clear to see where Finjan got his ideas from when we look at what he exclaimed as follows:

"Perhaps many of the people of the Dhi Qar Government do not know that the first airport to be built on planet Earth, 5,000 years ago, before the Christian era, was built here, in Dhi Qar. If you do not believe me, read the book of the great historian Zecharia Sitchin, who was an expert on Sumerian studies, read the books of Samuel Kramer ..."

Finjan quotes Sitchin and Kramer as his sources. Kramer was a professional, pioneering Assyriologist who researched and explained the amazing Sumerian culture to the Western world through the various tablets that were freshly found about half a century before his time. The works of Kramer and many of the other pioneering Assyriologists detailed how the Sumerian culture was the start of our civilized history. Sitchin, however, was a speculative writer on ancient history. He took everything we knew about the ancient world and wove together a story that could explain the enigmatic similarities in all the lost and forgotten civilizations like that of the Sumerians, Egyptians, and Mayans. It was Sitchin who theorized that the gods of old, mentioned in all major cultures, were the Sumerian Anunnaki, a race of extraterrestrials that traveled here in a distant past and genetically engineered Homo sapiens. It was Sitchin's work that caused Finjan to believe in what he said.

Saddam Hussein, Iraq's militant dictator from 1979–2003, was adamant about rebuilding and reinstating ancient Iraqi structures and pride. Iraq was not only home to Sumer but also the aggressive Babylonian kingdom. After the first Gulf War, Saddam campaigned to rebuild "Babylon," refurbishing some of Iraq's ancient monuments and also recreating some with new construction. In a propaganda piece issued from the Iraqi government during his early rule titled *From Nebuchadnezzar to Saddam Hussein, Babylon Rises Again*, we see the fervor as stated:

"Saddam Hussein emerges from Mesopotamia, as Hammurabi and Nebuchadnezzar had emerged … Saddam Hussein, the grandson of the Babylonians, the son of this great land is leaving his fingerprints everywhere."

Saddam attempted to recreate the vigor of the past rulers with immense construction projects, venerating him as the honorable head of the land. In a 1990 release from *World Press Review*, it was detailed that thousands of workers were employed to build the new Babylon, which was hopefully to be finished by 1994. Of course, Hussein was taken down, executed and his empire toppled after the infamous 9/11 attack in America, which he was subsequently tied to. What is important to take away from this story is that the pride and effort, whether destructive or not, that Hussein had in rebuilding the ancient past of Babylon caused a messianic frenzy in Christian America.

In a 2003 article, written right at the onset of the Iraq War after the 9/11 attacks, by professional newspaper commentator Jack Van Ens titled "Why President Bush Blasts Babylon," we received some interesting facts about Christian America at the time. Van Ens details that a Gallup poll at the time showed that 46 percent of

Americans identified as "born again" or "evangelical Christians." That was about half of the country! In a 1999 statistic by *Newsweek* magazine, it was shown that 40 percent of Americans believed in and were awaiting an end-times apocalypse. President George W. Bush, leader during the 9/11 attacks and early Iraq War, gained massive support from Christian America. Preying on the hearts and minds of the people Bush would often show Christian sentiments for his actions. Palestinian delegate at the time, Nabil Shaath, is quoted in a 2005 article by *The Guardian* as saying of Bush's Christian paranoia:

"President Bush said to all of us: 'I am driven with a mission from God.' God would tell me, 'George go and fight these terrorists in Afghanistan.' And I did. And then God would tell me 'George, go and end the tyranny in Iraq.' And I did."

In what has now become known as the "Land Letter," President of the Ethics & Religious Liberty Commission and Southern Baptist Convention, Richard D. Land and four other major evangelical leaders at the time sent a signed a letter to Bush in favor of his plans for the war in Iraq. Together the five evangelicals had a massive following, which we can assume covered that 40 percent of America at the time that was awaiting an end-times war. All of this end-times scare that still exist today, comes from the enigmatic Book of Revelation by Saint John the Apostle. Being the last book in the New Testament, it prophesizes the coming of the Messiah, the rising of "Mystery Babylon," a war of Armageddon, and the Apocalypse, where a revealing of all truth occurs and everyone is judged. Throughout the New Testament there are hints of end-times "signs," which are to appear to warn believers of the final showdown. One of these signs is the ominous "wars and rumors of war," which is taken from Mathew 24, wherein Jesus tells us that after this sign, his return is imminent. Many American Christians at the time of Saddam's endeavors to rebuild Babylon saw this and the onset of war as a sure sign that the end was near and that they and America were on the side of God in the battle of Armageddon.

The passion for Christianity in America still bustles as evangelicals see themselves as players in a war of good versus evil. For many years theologians let alone Christians had no full idea as to how its entire religion, based on Judaism, was subsequently based on much more ancient myths belonging to the Sumerians. This connection has come to fruition and respect over the years. The Bible Museum in Washington, DC, came under fire around 2017 when it was realized by Homeland Security that the museum had in its possession an infinitely valuable clay tablet that was stolen. This tablet, the 3,500-year-old "Gilgamesh Dream Tablet," belonged to a series of about seventeen thousand artifacts looted from Iraq and the Middle East during the Gulf and Iraq wars from 1991–2003. The Bible Museum acquired the tablet in 2014 for $1.6 million. After the lawsuits, the Museum owners paid out $3 million in settlements with the Justice Department, also returning thousands of other tablets.

Western Christians have a fascination with all things biblical and seem to be selective about what they adore and what they abhor about the Middle East. Since the finding of the Mesopotamian tablets in the nineteenth-century theologians have been eager to use their contents as being evidence for the veracity of the Bible. As far as the whole Iraq War, in retrospect with the final pulling out of our operations in the Middle East during the Biden administration, which to many was a climatic showcase of our arrogancy and chaotic mishandling of the entire ordeal, many have questioned the legitimacy of the entire endeavor. Along with the war, the frenzy of Christian end-times mongering proved to be exaggerated. Jesus never came back; Babylon wasn't rebuilt and yet the troubles of daily life continue for us all. Christians found it necessary to venerate the integral history of our Iraqi ancestors through the preservation of Mesopotamian tablets yet could care less to show real support to help our brothers and sisters living there now. I can assume that the many Christian leaders who now relish in the academic understanding of the importance the ancient Mesopotamian tablets had for the development of Judaism, do so to show how they bring veracity to their religion. The truth is actually the opposite. At every contextual corner Christians like to project their narrative onto biblical history, substituting ancient philosophies and myths with Jesus. They claim that all human history as presented in biblical stories is a preparation for the coming of Christ, his resurrection and eventual return. One remarkable example takes place in 1 Peter 3:18–20. Chapter 3 of 1 Peter is a list of philosophical sayings about doing what is right for God's sake even if you're under persecution as seen in verse 17:

"For it is better, if the will of God be so, that ye suffer for well doing, than for evil doing."—King James Bible

Verse 18 presents a crucial doctrine in the mainframe of Western Christianity, the doctrine that Christ saved prejudgment souls from Hell after his dying on the cross. An online article from Christianity.com, which we can assume holds the same belief as most Western Christians, states:

"In traditional Christian theology, the Harrowing of Hell, or 'the descent of Christ into Hell' or Hades, is the saving act of Christ to the souls in Hades between His Crucifixion and Resurrection. In triumphant descent, Christ preached and bestowed salvation to the souls held captive there since the beginning of the world … The most cited Bible passage for the account of Jesus descending to hell before His resurrection is 1 Peter 3:18–20."

Verse 18–20 states:

"For Christ also suffered once for sins, the righteous for the unrighteous, to bring you to God. He was put to death in the body but made alive in the Spirit. After being made alive, he went and made proclamation to the imprisoned spirits to those who were disobedient long ago when God waited patiently in the days of Noah while the ark was being built. In it only a few people, eight in all, were saved through water ..."—KJV

Again, this is an integral part of Christian doctrine; it is scriptural evidence for the death and resurrection of Christ and also that he descended into "Hell" and redeemed ancient souls there. However, the word translated isn't Hell but prison. It is misleading to preach that this verse is evidence for Hell. These verses have intrigued theologians and Bible scholars for hundreds of years. It is powerful yet strange and almost contradictory to the rest of the Christian religion. Some have used it as evidence that Christ did not rise physically after his crucifixion for the verse clearly states that he rose in the "spirit."

In a thesis submitted in 2002, to Liberty University for a degree in Master of Arts by Jason M. Hauffe titled "Interpretation of 1 Peter 3:18–22," we learn some key points as to why this section of the Bible is theologically strange. Hauffe starts by saying of the verses:

"The exegesis of 1 Peter 3: 18–22 is a seemingly endless labyrinth of closely-knit problems that has puzzled and motivated many. All who have attempted to unravel its secrets have soon realized that it is a notoriously difficult passage to interpret."

He's of course not the only scholar to recognize the conundrum in those verses. Martin Luther, the pioneer of the Protestant Reformation, is quoted as saying:

"A wonderful text is this, and a more obscure passage perhaps than any other in the Testament, so that I do not know for a certainty just what Peter means … I cannot understand and I cannot explain it. And there has been no one who has explained it."

The first among the early Church to interpret the verses was Clement of Alexandria. He, like his contemporaries who followed, viewed them as clearly stating that Christ spent some time during the intermediate three days of his death to preach to the prejudgment souls in "Hades" to "set the captives free." These souls from Noah's time of course didn't know about Christ and his divine revelation so the early theologians saw that it must have been necessary for Christ to go and evangelize to them. The verses generally from 18–22 are confusing to Christians because they do not provide a detailed explanation as to what Peter is talking about. The basic questions theologians wrestle with as seen in D. N. Campbell and

Fika J. van Rensburg's paper "A History of the

Interpretation of 1 Peter 3:18–22" are:

"Who are the spirits in prison? Where is the prison located? What

did Christ actually proclaim? And: When did this preaching take

place?"

All of the confusion and various interpretations of the

verses could be caused by what other scholars say has

come about due to an emendation of some of the original

Greek words used in 1 Peter 3:18–20. The strange

account of Christ's spirit going to a "prison" and

preaching to the disobedient spirits of Noah's time are

also made clear when we understand that the basis for

this seemingly allegorical philosophy is the Book of

Enoch.

In verse 3:18 we see Peter telling us that Christ suffered "for sins, the just for the unjust, that he might bring us to God ..." And then he continues to say that Christ died and was resurrected as a spirit. In verse 19 is where the confusion begins as it states: "By which also he went and preached unto the spirits in prison ..." Mainstream theologians see this as a clear contextual thought as Christ being the one who went to preach to the spirits but as briefly reviewed above, this causes major doctrinal confusion. In the original Greek the opening of verse 19, which is sometimes translated as (by which) or (in which), initially read ENOKAI, is really close to ENOX (Enoch) in Greek. If we add a Greek chi to ENΩKAI, "in which also," it transforms into ENΩXKAI, (and Enoch). A line of scholars going over hundreds of years have made claims that not only was passage 19–20 referring to the

Book of Enoch but that Enoch's name was incidentally left out.

The first scholar to translate the original Greek manuscript words of 1 Peter from Christ to Enoch was William Bowyer. Bowyer published his second translation of the Greek New Testament in 1772. In his translation he substituted Enoch as the figure of context in verse 19 instead of Christ. Bowyer had a strong understanding of early Christianity and translation, for the Book of Enoch had yet to be rediscovered by Westerners let alone translated. It wouldn't be until 1821 that the first English translation of the Book of Enoch would be published. Later scholars in the early twentieth century would also follow this line of thinking. J. R. Harris, a biblical scholar living from 1852–1941, also wrote about what to him was the obvious reference to Enoch in 1 Peter. Harris was instrumental in discovering and translating ancient biblical manuscripts from the Sinai area. He was a boots-on-the-ground scholar who understood ancient biblical context. In his 1891 essay for *Expositor*, "A Further Note on the use of Enoch in 1 Peter," he detailed the importance of the missing context. In his essay he briefly explains:

"These imprisoned spirits are the angels who sinned with mortal women, for whose offence and its punishment the book of Enoch is our prime authority. The very language used in Enoch for their place of punishment—'This place is the prison of the angels' (Enoch xxi. 10)—is in close correspondence with the Petrine expression."

Harris believed as those in his line of thinking that there could have been an honest omission of Enoch's name out of the opening of the nineteenth verse because it was so similar to the other words that it was mistakenly erased as a repeated word by translators. When plugging Enoch back into the equation Harris points out that:

"Perhaps after all the difficulty really arises from the fact that the subject of the word [Enoch] has dropped out of the text, and that the real person who made proclamation to the spirits in prison is not Christ, but Enoch himself ..."

The reason these scholars saw the story of Enoch reflected in the enigmatic Petrine passage is that they understood that the Book of Enoch played an incalculable role in the philosophical development of the New Testament.

The Book of Enoch, as it's referred to, is actually a series of manuscripts all attributed to the patriarch Enoch.

These manuscripts span from the second century BCE up to the fifth century CE and possibly later. There are three "books" of Enoch titled 1 Enoch, 2 Enoch and 3 Enoch. The first of course contains the oldest fragments, going back to the first and second centuries BCE. The various fragments are written in different languages including that of Hebrew, Old Slavonic, and Ethiopic Ge'ez. Some of the manuscripts appear to be copies from other languages including Greek. Much of the contents are considered apocalyptic texts. They contain strange and daunting information about the nature of evil.

Enoch himself was the great-grandfather of Noah, the survivor of the flood. The Bible briefly mentions Enoch toward the end of Genesis 5, right before the famous flood story. The Bible simply states that:

"And all the days of Enoch were three hundred sixty and five years And Enoch walked with God: and he was not; for God took him."—KJV

There in Genesis 5 we get no explanation as to what is meant by Enoch being "taken" by God. He's among the few in the Bible including Elijah who are chosen to be lifted directly to Heaven. This strange excerpt might be referencing a much denser tale. What makes the various fragments of the Book of Enoch so special is that they expand on this enigmatic passage, giving us intense detail about Enoch's life and adventures before he disappears leaving behind mankind to endure the oncoming catalyst. The *Book of the Watchers,* a manuscript within 1 Enoch describes what was left out of the Bible's version of Enoch's story. In it a gang of "fallen angels" make a pact to stick together in rebelling against God. Among their treachery they teach humans various practices deemed immoral such as weapon making and the art of makeup as is seen in R. H. Charles's translation:

"And Azâzêl taught men to make swords, and knives, and shields, and breastplates, and made known to them the metals of the earth and the art of working them, and bracelets, and ornaments … And there arose much godlessness, and they committed fornication, and they were led astray, and became corrupt in all their ways."

It was these same Watchers who eventually snatched and mated with human women, creating the great abomination, their offspring the Nephilim. The story of angels mating with women and creating the Nephilim is also reflected in the Bible within Genesis 6. Again, like the tale of Enoch, the Bible's version is vague and short. As is seen in the Book of Enoch, God's true intent in allowing the Great Flood to sweep over mankind was to eliminate not just the corruption that had taken place but the offspring of the angels and women, the Nephilim. Also, in the Book of Enoch, we get more information about his disappearance with God. In 2 Enoch also known as the *Book of the Secrets of Enoch* we see this theme initiated as its opening lines attest:

"There was a wise man, a great artificer, and the Lord conceived love for him and received him, that he should behold the uppermost dwellings and be an eye-witness of the wise and great and inconceivable and immutable realm of God Almighty."

In the above quote the author is preparing us for the reason why Enoch was "taken" and thus causing his enigmatic disappearance in Genesis. The story continues with Enoch telling his side of the story saying:

"And there appeared to me two men, exceeding big, so that I never saw such on earth; their faces were shining like the sun ... those men said to me: Have courage, Enoch, do not fear; the eternal God sent us to you, and lo! You shalt to-day ascend with us into heaven ..."

We find out after reading 2 Enoch that he was chosen to be shown secrets of the universe. In 1 Enoch the story is also explained saying to us after he was taken that:

"Enoch disappeared and none of the sons of men knew where he was hidden, where he was, or what had happened ..."

Enoch was shown secrets and told prophecies of the coming flood of which he would have a chance to warn his descendants. Before returning to earth to be with his people one last time, he was told to speak to the

Watchers, the fallen angels, and to reprove them, as we see in this quote:

"Enoch, scribe of righteousness. Go and inform the Watchers of Heaven, who have left the High Heaven and the Holy Eternal Place, and have corrupted themselves with women, and have done as the sons of men do and have taken wives for themselves and have become completely corrupt on the earth. They will have on Earth, neither peace, nor forgiveness of sin, for they will not rejoice in their sons. The slaughter of their beloved ones they will see; and over the destruction of their sons they will lament and petition forever. But they will have neither mercy nor peace."

The Book of Enoch makes it clear that God's wrath was provoked by the doings of the fallen angels and that the Great Flood was brought forth to destroy and punish everyone involved. As for the fallen angels who initially rebelled, they were set to be imprisoned until the final judgment day. In their imprisonment is where Enoch visited them so that he could dictate their fate, relaying the message from the angels and God. All of this took place prior and during the "days of Noah."

It's clear to many scholars that the Book of Enoch was tantamount to the messianic development of early Christianity. We see direct parallels in 1 Peter to 1 Enoch as follows:

1 Peter 1:20

"He was destined before the foundation of the world but was revealed at the end of the ages for your sake."

1 Enoch 48:6–7a

"For this (reason) he was chosen and hidden in his presence before the world was created and forever. And the wisdom of the Lord of

Spirits has revealed him to the holy and the righteous; for he has preserved the lot of the righteous."

These verses speak of the messiah who is to be revealed to the world in the end of days with the former of course referring to Jesus. The Book of Enoch simply calls him "Son of Man," "Messiah of the Lord of Spirits." The final judgment in 1 Peter is apparently influenced from 1 Enoch as well as is seen here:

1 Peter 4:5

"But they will have to give an accounting to him who stands ready to judge the living and the dead."

1 Enoch 69:27

"And he sat on the throne of his glory, and the whole judgment was given to the Son of Man, and he will make sinners vanish and perish from the face of the earth."

It's clear the author of 1 Peter was aware of the Book of Enoch and at least impressed by it if not entirely moved by its apocalyptic messages. We can see now why scholars like Bowyer and J. R. Harris saw it fit to place Enoch as the figure of context in 1 Peter 3:19–20:

"After being made alive, he went and made proclamation to the imprisoned spirits, to those who were disobedient long ago when God waited patiently in the days of Noah …"

This passage as I've already explained has been translated by scholars with the inclusion of Enoch such as the "An American Translation (AAT), 1939":

"In it Enoch went and preached even to those spirits that were in prison, who had once been disobedient, when in Noah's time …"

Regardless of which translation is used, what is being said by Peter in this passage is that Christ died but was resurrected in spirit. In verse 19 it was in the same spirit (form, fashion, or process) in which either Jesus or Enoch went and preached to the lost souls from Noah's time. Whether Enoch was meant to be the figure of context in that passage or if Jesus was to be likened to Enoch in that passage, it's clear that Peter and that passage in particular, were expanding on the subject of immorality caused by the ancient days when the fallen angels were still around. The omission of the Enoch connection could have been a mistake, a misunderstanding, or a deliberate deletion. We may never really know what happened; however, there is no doubt that the Book of Enoch played an important role in how early Christianity formed. There are dubious details as to why Enoch was demoted over the centuries as a non-canonical book when it used to be held in such high regard.

As already mentioned, the Book of Enoch influenced Christian apocalyptic literature and the legend of the fallen angels. As Dr. R. H. Charles puts it, "the influence of Enoch on the New Testament has been greater than that of all the other apocryphal and pseudepigraphal books taken together" Dr. R. H. Charles was a theologian and Bible scholar (1855–1931) who wrote an extensive and authoritative work on the Book of Enoch and its importance in the old world of the early Judeo-Christian development. Paul the Apostle was seemingly well versed in the Book of Enoch and frequently made doctrinal statements that were based on the ancient book. As in his strange commandment in 1 Corinthians 11:10

where it is stated that women should "veil" their heads. The King James Version states:

"For this cause ought the woman to have power on her head because of the angels."

In other translations the word power is sometimes replaced with "covering." What is interesting is that Paul warns women to shield themselves when praying "because of the angels." He is most likely referring to the well-known story of his time of the fallen angels taking earthly women and mating with them, which in early Christianity was seen as the source of sin. Paul also indirectly quotes Enoch's prophetic visions when describing Christ in I Timothy 6:16:

"Who alone is immortal and who lives in unapproachable light, whom no one has seen or can see. To him be honor and might forever. Amen."—NIV

This description fits Enoch's vision of the messiah as follows:

"No angel was capable of penetrating to view the face of Him, the Glorious and the Effulgent; nor could any mortal behold Him. A fire was flaming around Him."

The Book of Enoch was important to early Christianity; Paul must have been aware of its daunting prophetic teachings. Although The Book of Enoch doesn't mention Christ by name, early Christians saw a definite connection and appropriated its contents. Luke 9:35 mentions:

"A voice came from the cloud, saying, 'This is my Son, whom I have chosen; listen to him.'"—NIV

Speaking of Christ as the Son in this passage Christians were linking age-old prophecies of a messiah with their leader; however, older versions differed on the word "Son." *The Pulpit Commentary* put together by The Reverend Joseph S. Exell and Henry Donald Maurice Spence-Jones, in 1899, declares that:

"The reading here of the older authorities must be adopted. Instead of the voice out of the cloud saying, 'This is my beloved Son,' we must substitute, 'This is my Elect.'"

This concept of the elect or "elect one" is central to the Book of Enoch, mentioned many times throughout the various texts such as this quote, "And in that place mine eyes saw the Elect One of righteousness and of faith …" The book of Jude in the New Testament blatantly quotes The Book of Enoch, stating,

"And Enoch … prophesied … saying, Behold, the Lord cometh with ten thousands of his saints …"

The Book of Enoch wasn't always placed as apocryphal or non-canonical. In the second century CE, Justin the Martyr (110–165 CE) wrote in his *Second Apology* some interesting points about the fallen angels, which followed a unique line of thinking prominent in the Book of Enoch. He states:

"They subsequently subjected the human race to themselves …

and among men they engendered murders, wars, adulteries, all

sorts of dissipation and every species of sin."

Justin was an early Christian philosopher who attempted

to appeal to Emperor Antoninus to cease his persecution

of the Christians. Justin was of course martyred, along

with some of his students.

Athenagoras, second-century Athenian Christian father,

wrote in his *Plea for the Christians* an excerpt about fallen

angels in which he is of course utilizing the specific tale of

Enoch as his source. In it he indirectly refers to Enoch as

a prophet. As is shown here:

"(You know that we say nothing without witnesses, but state the things which have been declared by the prophets); these [fallen angels] fell into impure love of virgins, and were subjugated by the flesh ... Of these lovers of virgins, therefore, were begotten those who are called giants."

Clement of Alexandria (ca. 150–215 CE), the integral early Christian theologian of Alexandria Egypt, wrote of the angels that they:

"Renounced the beauty of God for a beauty which fades, and so fell from heaven to earth."

Irenaeus, a second-century Greek bishop who was integral in creating the Catholic orthodoxy, spoke on Enoch and the fallen angels in his famous *Against Heresies*. In it he said:

"Enoch … God's legate to the angels although he was a man, and was translated, and is preserved until now as a witness of the just judgment of God, because the angels when they had transgressed fell to the earth for judgment, but the man who pleased [God] was translated for salvation …"

There we see Irenaeus declaring Enoch's imperative role as the God's legate with authority over the angels, referencing the famous story of him visiting them in a divine prison in the Book of Enoch. Enoch's interaction with angels good and bad is prevalent throughout his lore, as is seen in this quote from 2 Enoch:

"And I saw a darkness greater than earthly darkness. And there I perceived prisoners under guard, hanging up, waiting for the measureless judgment. And those angels have the appearance of darkness itself, more than earthly darkness. And unceasingly they made weeping, all the day long. And I said to the men who were with me, 'Why are these ones being tormented unceasingly?' Those men answered me, 'These are those who turned away from the Lord, who did not obey the Lord's commandments, but of their own will plotted together and turned away with their prince and with those who are under restraint in the fifth heaven.' And I felt very sorry for them; and those angels bowed down to me and said to me, 'Man of God, pray for us to the Lord!' And I answered them and said, 'Who am I, a mortal man, that I should pray for angels? Who knows where I am going and what will confront me? Or who indeed will pray for me?'"

Lactantius, (240–320 CE) prominent theologian and advisor to Constantine I, wrote of the fallen angels as well saying:

"God, in His foresight, sent angels for the protection and improvement of the human race ... However, while the angels lived among men, that most deceitful ruler of the earth, by his very association, gradually enticed them to vices and polluted them through sexual relations with women."

All of these quotations show a clear line of early Christian doctrine claiming that a majority of sin in the world began with the defilement of the fallen angels. The early Church believed that this defilement took place physically by corporal angels that descended upon earth. This tale was learned by the early Church fathers obviously by the Book of Enoch, written at least two hundred years before the Common Era.

Jesus in the New Testament is seemingly also aware of the Book of Enoch and paraphrases much of its apocalyptic teachings. As Christ makes it clear in his famous Sermon on the Mount: *"Think not that I am come to destroy the law, or the prophets: I am not come to destroy, but to fulfill."* Enoch, the great-grandfather of Noah, was indeed a prophet. When taken into biblical consideration, Enoch was probably above all the greatest prophet for he was not only absolved from death but spent time with the archangels, spoke to the fallen angels, prophesized about the flood, and was given privilege to see the messiah before all mankind and reside with him after he left earth. If any writings of the prophets were to be of importance to Jesus, I'm sure Enoch's would be at least considered. Following are some similarities between Christ's teachings and those of Enoch.

New Testament:

"Blessed are the meek: for they shall inherit the earth."

Enoch 6:9:

"The elect shall possess light, joy, and peace; and they shall inherit the earth."

New Testament:

"Woe unto that man by whom the Son of Man is betrayed! It had been good for that man if he had not been born."

Enoch:

"Where [is] the place of rest for those who have rejected the Lord of spirits? It would have been better for them; had they never been born."

New Testament:

"Woe unto you that are rich."

Enoch:

"Woe to you who are rich, for in your riches have you trusted."

Many theologians over the years have struggled with the obvious precedents in Christ's teachings found in the Book of Enoch, which spans over two hundred years before his time. Prolific author on biblical topics William J. Deane wrote in his 1891 *Pseudepigrapha* about this conundrum:

"We are asked to believe that our Lord and his apostles, consciously or unconsciously, introduced into their speech and writings ideas and expressions most decidedly derived from Enoch."

Deane was upset at the evolving view of early Christianity as much of his contemporaries probably were. The fact that the New Testament so heavily relied on the Book of Enoch for its philosophical and apocalyptic teachings in some ways discredits the uniqueness of it. Deane goes on to say in his work that he believes there is a conspiracy to deliberately devalue the "superhuman origin of

Christianity." The Book of Enoch was eventually taken out of the canon for various reasons we can assume. One reason in particular that frustrated early Church fathers is that it spoke about fallen angels being corporeal and having physical, sexual relations with earth women. All throughout the Bible we see occasions that corroborate the existence of angels with physical humanlike bodies.

There is a story told in Genesis about Jacob, the famous forefather of the Israelites, wrestling with an angel. Theologians often describe this event as allegorical, meaning to present a doctrinal point that the Church at times struggles with God's plan. Nonetheless, the Bible strangely describes this mysterious being at first as a "man." As is stated here:

"So, Jacob was left alone, and a man wrestled with him till daybreak … Then the man said, 'Let me go, for it is daybreak.' But Jacob replied, 'I will not let you go unless you bless me.'"

After the event, the "man" leaves after blessing Jacob. Jacob is stunned by this occurrence as is stated:

"Then he blessed him there. So, Jacob called the place Peniel, saying, 'It is because I saw God face to face, and yet my life was spared.'"

It is apparent that this man is an angel in disguise. In the later version in Hosea, that being is referred to as "God" and an "angel." Apparently, this being was divine at the very least. Another strange occurrence of corporeal angels takes place in the tale of Sodom and Gomorrah. At the time God was to destroy the two cities for being sinful. In the story Abraham pleads with God in an attempt to spare their lives. In the tale God declares that none should be spared, and that Abraham should hurry and take his family out of that place so that they can be saved from the fiery destruction soon to take place. Interestingly though it's not actually God who convenes on the matter directly. Three "angels" are sent two warn Abraham of the matter. As is told in Genesis 18, these angels, however, appear as men. They warn Abraham that they were sent to judge Sodom and Gomorrah, to decide whether or not to destroy it. As is seen in these passages:

"Abraham looked up and saw three men standing nearby. When he saw them, he hurried from the entrance of his tent to meet them and bowed low to the ground … Then the Lord said, 'Shall I hide from Abraham what I am about to do?' […] 'The outcry against Sodom and Gomorrah is so great and their sin so grievous that I will go down and see if what they have done is as bad as the outcry that has reached me. If not, I will know.'"

In the story these angels or emissaries are divine beings in human form sitting with Abraham sharing a meal, discussing whether or not the sinful cities should be destroyed. They are obviously human in appearance with a divine trait, so much so that the licentious people of Sodom take notice of their beautiful stature and mob after them. Pathetically, the mob of people is after the two divine emissaries so that they can have sex with them. As is seen here:

"The men of the city, even the men of Sodom, compassed the house round, both old and young, all the people from every quarter: And they called unto Lot, and said unto him, Where are the men which came into thee this night? bring them out unto us, that we may know them ..."—KJV

The phrase so "that we may know them" means so that we may have sex with them. To "know" someone is an archaic way of saying to have sex with someone. Later in Genesis 19, Abraham's nephew hides and protects the two angels in his home, where they further discussed the important issue. It's a strange tale that adds to the early Judeo-Christian belief in angels being able to take physical humanlike shape.

Zecharia Sitchin, famous author of Ancient Alien subjects who pioneered the Anunnaki theory, wrote about this account saying that these two men were none other than Anunnaki. He believed that all the biblical mentions of angels and the like were renditions of the Anunnaki. Even further than that he believed that the Bible was a summarization of ancient Mesopotamian tales about the Anunnaki. In the third book of his *Earth Chronicles* series, he details how a few ancient Mesopotamian texts hold what could be source mythology for the later story in Genesis. Sitchin's claims all stand on the contention that the story of man's creation in Genesis 1:26 was attributed to a group of beings as opposed to the religiously instituted God. As I've already explained in chapter 2 the word used in Genesis 1:26 when man was being created was "Elohim," which in Hebrew should be interpreted as plural. Interestingly in Genesis 19:29 after the destruction of Sodom in Gomorrah, we find the word Elohim again in the Hebrew script. It is the Elohim whom the destruction is attributed to. Reading from a Hebrew-English interlinear Bible from scripture4all.org we find the side-by-side translations as reading:

English

"And it came to pass, when God destroyed the cities of the plain, that God remembered Abraham ..."

Hebrew transliteration

"And he is becoming, into ruin of, Elohim, cities of the basin, and he is remembering, Elohim, Abraham ..."

Now of course in this passage Elohim is followed by singular context unlike the verses in Genesis 1:26. The convoluted meanings of words, context and changing of identifiers throughout the Bible make room for a lot of conjecture. We can't entirely agree that in this passage it was the Elohim in the plural that destroyed the sinful cities. However, when we take into consideration the story told previously in Genesis 18, it is apparent that it was the Elohim (angels) that did so. Abraham was specifically met by three angels who told him that they were sent to judge and destroy the cities. Sitchin links the story in the Bible to what is known as the Erra and Ishum text, also known as the Erra Epic. It is a Babylonian epic written in Akkadian with its oldest manuscripts dated from at least the seventh century BCE. Some scholars believe it could be several hundreds of years older. It's a tale of war and destruction, specifically of cities and its peoples who are disruptive and found useless to Erra. Erra is the main character in the story along with his companion Ishum and the supporting character Marduk. Erra, as has been concluded by many scholars in the field of Mesopotamian studies, is another name for the famed god Nergal. Ishum on the other hand isn't equally agreed upon to blatantly represent another well-known deity. Sitchin makes the claim that Ishum is another name for the Sumerian god Ninurta. There is some case for this claim; the epic opens up with Erra praising and greeting Ishum as: "O Hendursagga, first born of Enlil ..." Ninurta of course was the firstborn son of Enlil, a mighty warrior as is seen in various other texts from ancient Mesopotamia. Both Nergal and Ninurta are sons of the olden god Enlil, a part of the holy triad consisting of Anu, Enki and Enlil. In the epic it is these two gods who contemplate on destroying the cities of their rival Marduk. Throughout the tablets Erra is pacing and pondering, trying to convince himself to go forth with his plans of destruction. Throughout the soliloquies Erra turns to Ishum for advice and even his "seven weapons" who are personified as a reflection of Erra's mind. Reading from Benjamin R. Foster's 1995 translation we find this stated as follows:

"The Seven offer the encouragement that Erra needs. In a rousing call to arms, they extol the heroic excitement of the campaign, the honor, prestige and gratification it brings. The Seven claim vaguely that they are not respected enough, that others are growing more important than they ... 'Be off to the field, warrior Erra, make your weapons clatter, Make loud your battle cry that all around they quake, Let the Igigi-gods hear and extol your name, Let the Anunna-gods hear and flinch at the mention of your [name] ...'"

Now where Sitchin sees this story as a precedent to the Sodom and Gomorrah story is in a following section where Ishum intervenes in Erra's contemplation, just as

Abraham did so with the angels, attempting to stop the madness from ensuing. As is seen here:

"When Ishum heard what he said, he felt pity and said to the warrior Erra: 'O Lord Erra, why have you plotted evil against the gods? To lay waste the lands and decimate the people.'"

This is reminiscent of Abraham's plea for the cities as seen in Genesis 18:23–24:

"Then Abraham approached him and said: 'Will you sweep away the righteous with the wicked? What if there are fifty righteous people in the city? Will you really sweep it away and not spare[c] the place for the sake of the fifty righteous people in it?'"

Erra is annoyed by Ishum's hesitancy to save the people in a last-ditch effort as is seen in the following verses:

"Keep quiet, Ishum, listen to what I say, as concerns the people of the inhabited world, whom you would spare."

Eventually Erra is convinced of his evil urge and sets out to destroy the cities of Babylon belonging to Marduk, destroying them in a flash leaving everything desolate as is told here:

"I will make Marduk angry, stir him from his dwelling, and lay waste the people! ... Ill winds rose, and the bright daylight was turned to gloom, The clamor of the peoples throughout the land was stilled ..."

The two gods Erra and Ishum are viewed by Sitchin to be the two angels who enter the city of Sodom, who consult with Abraham's nephew Lot. As seen in Genesis 19:

"The two angels arrived at Sodom in the evening, and Lot was sitting in the gateway of the city. When he saw them, he got up to meet them and bowed down with his face to the ground."

I don't entirely agree with Sitchin's conclusion that the Erra Epic is the source for the Sodom and Gomorrah tale. However, it is interesting that in the Bible there are a few angels (Elohim) who are sent to survey and destroy the sinful cities and that in the Erra Epic we see something similarly reflected. What is important to take away from all of this is that the Bible was not shy in presenting physical angels who played integral roles in human affairs. That is what is most intriguing about the

Genesis stories, which do hold many other blatant influences from Sumerian tales as I've gone over in previous chapters. The Old Testament was written with actual history in mind but from an exaggerated Jewish perspective. The authors took the thousands of years of human history prior to them and summarized it, condensing the myths into simple forms that suited their narrative. This is evident in the case of the event of King Cyrus freeing the Jews from Babylonian captivity. As I detailed in an earlier chapter, the Bible relates that Cyrus did so after being inspired by Yahweh. However, the historical record as reported by the Cyrus Cylinder found in the nineteenth century reveals that Cyrus declared he was inspired by his patron deity Marduk. So again, the Jews rewrote history in favor of their narrative.

Returning to the Book of Enoch, its contents were problematic for the evolving institution of Christianity. It was problematic for one; it contained many passages that obviously influenced the New Testament and the teachings of Christ. It also contained the idea of angels being corporeal, which the Church was looking to do away with. Important early Christian scholar Julius Africanus (160–240 CE) was among the first to discredit the claim of fallen angels having sex with human women. He wrote about it in his large five-volume work known as the *Chronography*. He began what is known as the Sethite theory, which claims that the "sons of God" in the Genesis 6 story who mate with human women were actually the sons of Seth. He explains this as follows:

"The descendants of Seth are called the sons of God on account of the righteous men and patriarchs who have sprung from him, even down to the Saviour Himself; but that the descendants of Cain are named the seed of men, as having nothing divine in them, on account of the wickedness of their race and the inequality of their nature, being a mixed people, and having stirred the indignation of God."

This was a technicality that played on philosophy rather than academic integrity. The words used in Hebrew for "sons of God" is *B'nai ha Elohim*. Elohim as we've seen is cognate to the word *angels*. Elohim is only used in reference throughout the entire Bible toward God or his emissaries. The tale is obviously about the abomination that occurred when the divine lowered itself into grotesque form to mate with humans. Jerome, the famous translator of the Latin Vulgate, which was to be used as the Roman Catholic version of the Bible, wrote about the Book of Enoch as well. Jerome downplayed its importance, linking it to a blasphemous and heretical mystic of his time, Mani. Mani was the founder of Manichaeism, which was a blend of Christian, Gnostic, and pagan beliefs. Jerome said of the Book of Enoch:

"This book is quite explicit and is classified as apocryphal. The ancient exegetes have at various times referred to it, but we are citing it, not as authoritative, but merely to bring it to your attention ... Do you detect the source of the teachings of Manichaeus the ignorant?"

Church father of the late third century John Chrysostom, archbishop of Constantinople, wrote on this matter as well in his *Homilies on Genesis* saying:

"They say that it is not men that are referred to here, but angels, and that it is the angels that are called 'sons of God' ... It would be folly to accept such insane blasphemy."

Trailblazing Church father Saint Augustine is held as one of the most important Church scholars and philosophers living from 354–430 CE. He shaped Christianity in unprecedented ways with his theology. Another famous Church father and translator of the Latin Vulgate, Jerome, wrote to Augustine in 418 saying:

"You are known throughout the world; Catholics honour and esteem you as the one who has established anew the ancient Faith."

Augustine wrote in his epic *City of God*:

"I could by no means believe that God's holy angels could at that time have so fallen ... Let us omit then, the fables of those Scriptures which are called apocryphal, because their obscure origin was unknown to the fathers from whom the authority of the true scriptures have been transmitted to us by a most certain and well ascertained succession ... We cannot deny that Enoch, the 7th from Adam, left some divine writings, for this is asserted by the apostle Jude in his canonical epistle. But it is not without reason that these writings have no place in that Canon of scripture which was preserved in the temple of the Hebrew people by the diligence of successive priest; for their antiquity brought them under suspicion ..."

Augustine therefore refuses to believe that God's angels could reduce themselves to such lowly behavior as to incarnate and mate with earth women. He acknowledges that the writings of Enoch were monumental in influencing the New Testament, specifically in the book of Jude, but doubts the actual Book of Enoch's authenticity. Augustine sees the Jewish community as suspect, blaming them for the circulation of the apocryphal works of Enoch, deeming them heretical. Augustine alone, especially with his contemporaries would be enough to change the course of Christian thought and because of their denouncement of the Book of Enoch, it wouldn't be long before the Church fell out of favor with its manuscripts.

Over time the Church progressed away from the idea of corporeal angels who had sex with earth women. They might have done so to simplify their teachings, to make everything compatible and easily explainable. To the

Church today it doesn't seem as if the historical truth of things matters much as long as seats are filled, and people are convinced of the need to follow Jesus to avoid Hell. All the while this transaction is being handled by the clergy on the sly. The Church needs reasons to exist, reasons to justify what it does. The institution of Christianity, officialized in Rome by Constantine and the Council of Nicaea, is a major force in our world today. Overall, religion in general keeps many people in check; it's used as a social construct to provide organization to a mass of desperate folks with a gaping guilt needing to be patched. Religion in some horrible cases is even a pseudo branch of government, controlling how we conduct ourselves, affecting lives with forced dogma. Monotheism allows for things to be simple and easily controllable. Human history consists of chaos with daring kings, queens and warriors taking on the task of uniting the people under one banner. Not a single kingdom has been able to hold the reins forever; time and time again another comes by and destroys it, replacing the ways of old. Sumer started off as warring city-states, being overtaken by Sargon who instituted a form of monotheism where Inanna was the head deity. The Akkadian Empire was overrun by the Gutians and nearby nomads who again instituted a plethora of beliefs. Eventually came the Kingdom of Babylon, which conquered and constrained Mesopotamia under one rule with Marduk as its patron deity. During this era the Jews were held under captivity. It would be King Cyrus who would come along and defeat the Babylonians and institute religious tolerance, allowing the Jews to go back to their homeland and fortify their religion. It was after the exile that Judaism strengthened with the worship of Yahweh. Then came the Greeks and Romans who blurred everything with syncretism, allowing paganism to flourish once more. The difficult task of attempting to rule the known world at that time seemed impossible with all of the warring ideologies, to which each constituent of the kingdom was individually loyal. Christianity was necessary to institute as a universal religion, to unify and control the masses. The Book of Enoch held archaic ideas, ones that didn't suit the agenda of Christianity where Christ was unique and divine. The Church didn't want a political Jesus; they wanted a distant divine Jesus in which they were the mediators. The Book of Enoch undermines the Church. The power the Church has today rode off the back of the early institution of

Christianity and its gripping and suffocating power through the advent of the Vatican and the Inquisition.

The Book of Enoch was a bridge between the Jewish world and the new fanatical Christian world. We need not go into extensive detail about just how much tension has existed between these two groups since their onset up to the very day. The Book of Enoch started off as a Jewish work, springing from mystical Judaism; however, it ended up in mystical sects of early Christianity such as those who authored the Dead Sea Scrolls. Because the strange manuscripts speak of a messiah and end times, it was particularly intriguing to early Christians. The book became too Christian for Jews and because it held archaic angelology belonging to mystical Judaism, it became too Jewish for the later Church. It ceased to serve a purpose for the evolving institutions of the monotheistic Judeo-Christian worlds.

Church father Tertullian spoke on this dichotomy:

"But since Enoch in the same Scripture has preached likewise concerning the Lord, nothing at all must be rejected by us which pertains to us; and we read that 'every Scripture suitable for edification is divinely inspired.' By the Jews it may now seem to have been rejected for that (very) reason, just like all the other (portions) nearly which tell of Christ …"

Here Tertullian points out the resistance and repulsion each other have toward accepting a universal doctrine. Each would like to remain separated in its own domain. Judaism likes to remain loyal to the Old Testament and Yahweh, where the Christians take it upon themselves to stand above them and condescendingly reject their beliefs for not accepting the "new covenant" or revelation of Christianity.

Of course, once Christianity took hold in the rising Western countries, initially setting off with Rome, it would go on to take over the world in many ways. Christianity has shaped our world greatly; some would even argue that history since the advent of Christianity has revolved around the Judeo-Christian worldview. Here in America, for example, as I'm writing this book, there is a major upheaval in our country having to do with pseudo-biblical matters. There has been an overturning of a sanctioned law known as Roe V. Wade, which protected legal abortions. It was overturned due to mostly an aggressive push by Republican Christians who view abortions as a sin. There's no need to go deeply into this; however, it should be apparent that Christianity along with Judaism and Islam have shaped and continue to shape our world in major ways, all contending for supremacy. Interestingly they all are apprehensive about investigating their polytheistic origins that sprung from the Sumerian worldview. Each of these religions falls under the category of the "Abrahamic religions."

Abraham is seen as the first Jew in the Torah. It is he who God makes his first covenant when he puts Abraham to the test when he asks him to sacrifice his son Isaac. God blessed Abraham and promised him a nation and that his descendants will also carry this blessing as is explicit in Genesis 12:1–3:

"Now the Lord said to Abram, 'Go from your country and your kindred and your father's house to the land that I will show you. And I will make of you a great nation, and I will bless you and make your name great, so that you will be a blessing. I will bless those who bless you, and him who dishonors you I will curse, and pin you all the families of the earth shall be blessed.'"

Thus, Abraham was the father of the Jews and the chosen people. In Christianity Abraham is regarded more so as the spiritual ancestor of the faith in which a tradition of faith began. As is said by Paul in Romans 4:5, Abraham is "the father of all that believe." In Islam Abraham is regarded as a Muslim and is held in high esteem is as seen in this quote from the Quran 3:65–38:

"The people who are worthiest of Abraham are those who followed him, together with this Prophet and the believers."

So, it seems without Abraham there wouldn't be a foundation of faith for either of these three religions to evolve from. Over the years there have been academic debates about the historicity of Abraham and among those, what interests this work more specifically is his place of origin. Fascinatingly, as has been pointed out by many theologians and scholars, Abraham was possibly born a Sumerian. Regardless of if he was a real person or not, the impact of his character was tantamount to the Abrahamic faiths. The Sumerian origin of Abraham is still debated, with scholars defending various interpretations of the semantics used in the Torah. What we know for sure is Abraham was from "Ur Kasdim," literally "Ur of the Chaldeans." Ur of course was a famous capital city of Sumer. The contention with the birthplace of Abraham is that the "Chaldeans" although seemingly referring to the Sumerians, aren't easily identifiable. Many scholars disagree on who the Chaldeans really were. Chaldea has also been taken to mean Babylon, which was just north of Sumer. Nonetheless Chaldea or the Chaldeans seems to generally refer to a general area and peoples of ancient Mesopotamia. For example, King Nebuchadnezzar, king of Babylon, is referred to as having an army of Chaldeans.

Abraham's story is important because he is at the head of an unfolding of monotheism, the worship of the sublime god Yahweh. This worship was not yet sanctified by the Jews. Abraham was called to leave his home and travel where he would be led to his destiny to lead the future

Jews to their homeland. Most scholars place Abraham's legendary life to have been around the early second millennium BCE. If this is so, then we can easily assume that the Mesopotamia Abraham was living in was still steep with polytheism that was influenced by its Sumerian forefathers. This is made apparent in the Bible in Joshua 24:2–3:

"Joshua said to all the people, 'This is what the Lord, the God of Israel, says: "Long ago your ancestors, including Terah the father of Abraham and Nahor, lived beyond the Euphrates River and worshiped other gods. But I took your father Abraham from the land beyond the Euphrates and led him throughout Canaan and gave him many descendants …"'"

In that passage Abraham's father, Terah, is mentioned as having worshiped "other" gods. These other gods are of course those of the late Akkadian and early Babylonian kingdoms. Some scholars point Abraham to a couple of centuries before the reign of Hammurabi who was the first recognizable Babylonian ruler. Some scholars place Abraham as being a contemporary of Hammurabi in the eighteenth century BCE (1700s). Either way having been a native of "Chaldea" and having obvious ties to polytheism from his forefathers, Abraham was a witness to the influence of the old-world Sumerian influence. As I've detailed in chapter 2, Hammurabi's famous law code began with a praise to the Anunnaki gods of Sumer as is repeated here:

"When Anu the Sublime, King of the Anunaki, and Bel, the lord of Heaven and earth, who decreed the fate of the land, assigned to Marduk, the over-ruling son of Ea, God of righteousness, dominion over earthly man, and made him great among the Igigi, they called

Babylon by his illustrious name, made it great on earth, and

founded an everlasting kingdom in it, whose foundations are laid so

solidly as those of heaven and earth; then Anu and Bel called by

name me, Hammurabi, the exalted prince, who feared God, to

bring about the rule of righteousness in the land ..."

It is clear that Judaism arose out of the remains of a

polytheistic world with devotional respects of the highest

order to the Anunnaki. The "other" gods that Abraham's

father Terah allegedly worshipped must have been the

Anunnaki. The entire premise of the Old Testament is

that there is but one God and that mankind should only

worship him and him alone. The Bible's plan through the

commandment of Yahweh was to phase out the other

gods and introduce monotheism. This is made explicit in

the verses of Exodus 20:

"Thou shalt have no other gods before me … thou shalt not bow down thyself unto them, nor serve them; for I Jehovah thy God am a jealous God …"

This God of the Bible was seemingly aware of the Anunnaki and wanted his people to divert their devotion and religious practices from them toward himself, Yahweh. Either this is the case or the priesthood that wrote down the Bible wanted the people to do so. If that's the case, then they were attempting to simplify the structure of society to make it easily governable.

The Bible itself makes it clear that prior to the scriptures being put together into the Torah there was chaos and the worship of many gods. As I also briefly detailed in chapter 1, this is expressed in the book of Jeremiah 11:

"There is a conspiracy among the people of Judah and those who live in Jerusalem. They have returned to the sins of their ancestors, who refused to listen to my words. They have followed other gods to serve them … You, Judah, have as many gods as you have towns; and the altars you have set up to burn incense to that shameful god Baal are as many as the streets of Jerusalem …"

Jeremiah was among the last of the prophets before the Jews were overtaken by the Babylonians and taken into captivity. It would be in their captivity that they would find the strength and need to unify under a system of strict monotheism. It's interesting that the above passage mentions that the people of Judah had "returned to the sins of their ancestors …," meaning that they reverted to worshipping the gods of old, presumably the Anunnaki.

The origins of the Israelites (early Jews) were born out of the old world of Canaan. Early Hebrew is closely related to the Canaanite languages of old including Phoenician. It would be the Phoenician script that old Hebrew would be born out of in the ninth century. This is also expressed in the Old Testament in Isaiah 19:18:

"In that day five of Egypt's cities will follow the LORD of Heaven's Armies. They will even begin to speak Hebrew, the language of Canaan …"

In the old world of the Levant that the Israelites sprung from, there was a multitude of gods. The God that the

Jews later adopted as Yahweh, taken to be the sole Creator of all things, was subsequently worshipped by other groups as well. The Israelites adopted this deity and propped him to be their God. One the earliest mention of Yahweh outside of the Bible occurs in the Moabite Stone also known as the Mesha Stele. It was discovered in 1868 in Jordan. Written in the ninth century BCE, the inscription has many important aspects that verify biblical history. It mentions Israel and possibly the title "House of David." It was written by a King Mesha of Moab (Jordan). In the text he boasts of some military accomplishments, among those being the subjugation of the Israelites and taking the vessels or artifacts of Yahweh to his God's altar as a symbol of submission. As is seen in K. C. Hanson's 1969 translation:

"And from there I took Yahweh's vessels, and I presented them before Kemosh's face."

Older than this mention of Yahweh we have an inscription in a temple built by Amenhotep III (1386–1353 BCE). In this inscription we find again a boasting of military subjugation where the "Shasu of Yaheweh" are taken in as prisoners. The Shasu, however, are remembered as nomadic people of the ancient Southern Levant. Possibly a precursor to the Israelites, they are definitely different in their own right. From this inscription we can assume Yahweh was appropriated by the wandering Jews in the lands of Canaan during the time of Moses. Moses was the of the thirteenth generation after Adam and interestingly the name of God wasn't revealed until the time of Moses. While Moses was in exile from Egypt with his people it was on mount Horeb, while in contemplation, that Moses was visited by God. In that instance God revealed himself to Moses and also gave him his holy name, Yahweh. As is attested in Exodus 3:15 when Moses asks the sublime the God what he should call him:

"And God said moreover unto Moses, Thus shalt thou say unto the children of Israel, The Lord (Yahweh) God of your fathers, the God of Abraham, the God of Isaac, and the God of Jacob, hath sent me unto you …"

Scholars have attempted to find the source for the name Yahweh, going through various theories over the centuries. Professor Lewis Bayles Patton briefly detailed the various theories scholars have put forth in his 1906,

The Worship Yahweh-Worship in Israel. Patton explains that Yahweh is not originally Hebrew saying that

"The form Yahweh is not Hebrew, and is unintelligible to Hebrew ears. The interpretation 'He will be' is artificial, since in Hebrew this would be Yihyeh ..."

Patton argues that as Moses was wandering the desert of the Sinai where he was eventually led to the holy mountain. It was there that the Israelites assimilated a known god in the region. Patton elucidates this in the following passage:

"Horeb was already the 'mountain of God,' according to Exod. 3: I (E), before Moses received there his revelation. In 3:I2 (E) Yahweh says: 'When thou hast brought forth the children of Israel out of Egypt, ye shall serve God upon this mountain.' This implies that

Horeb is a sanctuary where the worship of Yahweh is already established. In I9:IO (E) the people on arriving at Horeb sanctify themselves and wash their clothes, as men were accustomed to do when visiting a holy place ..."

Patton suggests that Yahweh was a desert cult god that was appropriated by the wandering Israelites. This idea belongs to a centuries-old theory known as the "Kenite" theory. This theory postulates that Moses learned of Yahweh from the Midianite/Kenite priest of the Sinai area. The Bible holds some evidence for this as Patton greatly details in his essay, as shown in this passage:

"Yahweh says, when Israel arrives at Sinai: 'I have
 brought you to myself.' Such statements are inconsistent with the theory that Sinai first became a sanctuary of Yahweh in consequence of the revelation of Moses; they show that it was

already a holy place in pre-Mosaic times. But, as we have seen, Israel did not worship Yahweh before the exodus, and there is no tradition connecting it with Sinai before the time of Moses; consequently, Yahweh must have been the God of the people inhabiting Mount Sinai before the arrival of Israel."

There is also an eighth-century BCE inscription that was found in the Sinai area known as the Kuntillet Ajrud where the name of Yahweh is found alongside other ancient Canaanite deities. The short remaining legible sentences mention Yahweh as in this passage:

"I bless you by YHWH of Teman and by Asheratah. May he bless and keep you, and may he be with my lord forever."

Out of all of the basic information, evidence, and theories, it's apparent that the name Yahweh, the later supreme deity of Judaism, was adopted in the Sinai area by the early Israelites. When they were a nomadic tribe, they could have come into contact with other ally tribes that influenced this worship. Beside this point it's important to realize that the early Israelites were definitely born out of the polytheistic/henotheistic beliefs of the old world. It's been agreed upon by scholars that the god of the ancient Jews, Yahweh was a somewhat reimagined version of the Canaanite El, the head of the old-world pantheon. The Bible makes this clear in Exodus 6:2 when Yahweh is conversing and revealing wisdom to Moses:

"And God said to Moses, 'I am Yahweh—"the Lord." I appeared to Abraham, to Isaac, and to Jacob as El-Shaddai—"God Almighty"—but I did not reveal my name, Yahweh, to them.'"

El Shaddai (God Almighty) is a term that belongs to the more archaic category of names used for god prior to the usage of Yahweh. This category is a part of the prefix El category. The phonetic usage of the word El (God) goes back to at least Akkadian times with the form Il. As Frank Moore Cross examines in great detail in his 1973 *Canaanite Myth and Hebrew Epic,* Il is also pronounced throughout the old world as Ilu, Ilum, and Ilah. All of these being antecedent to the El, which was the later fortified version. From these root words we can assume the pattern was followed into the early Arabic world where the name Allah was eventually formed out of.

As mentioned before, once the Jews were held captive in Babylon and then set free by Cyrus the Persian, they then decided it would be necessary to strengthen themselves under the institution of Judaism through the Torah and monotheism. During the fifth century BCE while Artaxerxes was ruling the new Persian Empire, there was upheaval throughout the empire within cultural groups with contradictory ideologies to that of the overall empire. The priests Ezra and Nehemiah were chosen among the royal court of the Persian kingdom to be mediators to the Jewish community and organize them under a local cultural law that they could follow. In Ezra 7 of the Old Testament there is a letter from Artaxerxes reproduced giving Ezra permission and command to quell and organize his people saying:

"To Ezra the priest, who has studied very well the law of the God of heaven. I hope that you are well ... I have given this command:

You have the law of your God that he has given to you ... Go and see if your people in Judah and Jerusalem are obeying his law ... Ezra, your God has helped you to be wise. So, you must choose judges and officers who know the laws of your God. Then they will decide things for all the people who live in the region on the west side of the Euphrates river. If the people do not know the laws of your God, you must teach them. Everyone must obey the laws of your God and also the laws of the king. If they do not obey, they deserve the right punishment ..."

It wasn't long after this that the institution of monotheism for the Jews began, ushering in a slow process that would overtake most of the Western world with its sequels in Christianity and Islam. The new religious institution with its priesthood would serve the Jews greatly throughout time as they stood amidst all the changes that occurred in the world, allowing them to evolve into a powerful community and country. After the Persians took over the Greeks would step in under Alexander the Macedonian. There is a legend told throughout rabbinical teachings about this transition of power and how it benefited the Jews. In a tenth-century work known as the *Book of Josippon*, we are told that among the first rabbi's there was the now famous and deeply beloved Shimon HaTzadik (Simon the Righteous). It was he who helped guide the modern historical Jewish community into the new world of the common era. When Alexander was stepping into Jerusalem during his conquest of the Persian Empire, we are told, he bowed down before HaTzadik in reverence saying that he had a vision of this leader and that in the vision it was revealed Alexander would succeed in his conquest. Already enjoying the religious and political tolerance under the Persians, the Jewish Temple was now elevated even more so and allowed to continue its presence among the evolving western kingdom. This respect would lead into the Hellenistic era where both cultures would mix and create new ethnicities and works of spiritual literature. The first foreign language the Old Testament was translated into was Greek. This was so to help bring some of the now Greek Jews and also non-Jews into the religion and community. The institution of monotheism would be strong, gaining a competitor in its sister religion Christianity, which the later "Gentile" or Western world would favor. The history of Christianity's monotheistic takeover is very similar to that of Judaism's. There is no need to go into the details, but it is well understood that the Greeks and Romans were pagans who would later adopt Christianity and convert to a monotheistic lifestyle. This was done so under the

Constantinian era which, like the Persian rulers before him, saw it necessary to unify the people under religious ideals. However, the Romans took this further and instead of allowing communities to just simply rule over themselves with their ancestorial religion, the Romans instituted a new state religion to phase out paganism and progress the world into a new indoctrination of one God, one kingdom. Once Islam blossomed and ravaged in its conquest as the new player on the scene then we had the three major Abrahamic religions contending for supremacy.

Truthfully it doesn't really matter which religion is correct; they all serve the same purpose, which is to unify the disorganized tribes into a country ruled under one god and one leader with its priesthood to mediate between the people and God. It's a simple way to quell and control the people. There is no need to examine either Christianity or Islam for historical veracity because both rely on Judaism and its mythology. Without Judaism neither would exist. As I've attempted to present throughout this entire work, Judaism wouldn't exist without the Sumerian mythology therefore the omitting of the Anunnaki from the religious doctrines is a deliberate shift into a new institution to indoctrinate and control the population that was once independent and non-reliant on the state. The formation of monotheism claims to benefit God; however, it ultimately benefits the priesthood and its political allies through the usage of mass organization and control.

Chapter 5

Conclusion

Truth is not what we wish it to be; it just is. It is our responsibility to learn the truth, no matter how difficult the task. Once we know it then we can freely decide what to believe whether for sincerity or for folly. Do not deceive yourself and think that just because you can make assumptions about something that what it is will be under your assumption. We must understand ancient knowledge not by what it means to us, but simply by what it means.

The origins of humanity as recorded by our ancestors began with the gods creating us in their image to be helpers in tending this world and to serve them. This history changed over time as we grew more intelligent with the way we organized our societies. We felt it necessary to centralize control and with that came the formation of monotheism. The religious would say that God is real and that we did descend from a divine being. They would also say that there is only one God, and all the rest are false gods or demons. The New Age and general occult would say something similar to this like there is a single source Creator and from it we emanated as souls only to forget our true nature. Both perspectives claim that this life is a sort of test in which we must purify ourselves to ascend back into the kingdom of "heaven." No one really knows. All we know is that we are here, and that life is more miraculous than we could ever account for. Some would say that our origins are deliberately kept hidden from us so that we don't wake up to who we are and how powerful we can really be against the institutions that control us. The mystery religions and occult systems like that of the Freemasons would say that the truth of our origins was lost to us through the cataclysms of the past like the Great Flood. After the cataclysms esoteric priesthoods were formed to preserve and transmit this information to later generations through various teachings and artifacts. There could be some truth to all of this.

Although the Sumerian culture consists of some of the world's oldest pieces of literature, it is not the oldest remnant of our civilized history. As I've mentioned previously, the oldest known piece of literature is the Sumerian Kesh temple hymn. In this text we find a strange recollection of the gods building some type of structure as seen here:

"House ... inspiring great awe, called with a mighty name by An; house ... whose fate is grandly determined by the Great Mountain Enlil! House of the Anuna gods possessing great power, which gives wisdom to the people; house, reposeful dwelling of the great gods! House, which was planned together with the plans of heaven and earth, ... with the pure divine powers; house which underpins the Land and supports the shrines! House, mountain of abundance which passes the days in glory ..."

The hymn also makes it clear that the main structure was used to hold sacred ceremonies as seen in the following passage:

"In the house the king places stone bowls in position; the good en priest ... holds the lead-rope dangling. The a-tu priests holds the staff; the ... brings the ... waters. The ... takes his seat in the holy place; the enkum priests bow down … The pacec priests beat the drumskins; they recite powerfully, powerfully."

—Oxford translation

For this to be the oldest piece of literature and to show an intelligent and delicate scenery should make it obvious that our culture as civilized people reaches further back than the history available to us. There is obviously much lost to us, a missing portion of our past that is veiled by the harsh conditions of life's cycles that breaks all things down, hidden in the strata of earth's mass.

Possibly the oldest mention of the Great Flood known to us comes from the Sumerian King List. The SKL is actually comprised of various manuscripts used to piece together the famous list of legendary rulers going far back into prehistoric times. First published in 1906, the list is famous for giving a total of about 432,000 years of rulership broken up by about 255 rulers. The numbers of years have been debated and speculated on. The list is spectacular with astronomical numbers for the years that some of the kings ruled. For example, we see in the Oxford online translation that the first ruler, Alulim, ruled for 28,800 years. The variable in question here is the word for "years" that is used in the original Sumerian. The word used is *shars*, which could be interpreted in different ways. The Sumerians based their mathematical computations on a sixty or sexagesimal system. This might have been chosen for religious purposes; however, it proved useful in daily life also. Much of the Sumerian tablets found are detailed records of transactions. They were meticulous about their financial and transactional record-keeping. Having a based sixty system could allow one to reduce units to very fine-tuned units (halves, thirds, quarters, fifths, sixths, tenths, twelfths, fifteenths, twentieths, and sixtieths) and still have them produced as whole numbers. This also allowed for small numbers to be quickly expressed as large quantities. As is exquisitely detailed by Raul Lopez in an essay titled "The Antediluvian Patriarchs and the Sumerian King List" from 1998, the Sumerians used a sequence of sixty to the power of other values:

"For the next power of the base (60^2), a large circle was used that was made by vertically pressing the larger end of the stylus into the clay. As with the symbol for 600, a small circle was impressed inside the larger circle (3,600) to multiply it by ten and represent 36,000. Although the Sumerian system had a sexagesimal base, the symbol for ten (the small circle) was used as an intermediate symbol between powers of sixty. This simplified the tallying procedure by grouping by ten the ciphers for the different powers. The resulting number was very easy to understand and used the *multiplicative* principle."

That pictorial style belonged to the earliest of Sumerian records. They would later develop a quicker, more script-like style of expressing the numbers in cuneiform. Some scholars would debate that the term *shar* when referring to the time frames for different rulers was misinterpreted and could be used interchangeably to denote different units. For example, in Alulim's case instead his rule being twenty-eight thousand years, which is 8 x 3,600, maybe he ruled for twenty-eight thousand shars (days), which would be 28,000/(Sumerian 360), equaling eighty years. This would have to be heavily studied and broken down; the later years down the list are much shorter, which couldn't be broken down by the same logic. For this reason, the list is deemed mythological or esoteric in its underlying content. What is important about it, particularly for this book is its mention of a "flood." With manuscripts going back to the third BCE, the best-preserved version of the SKL is the Weld-Blundel Prism. It is a rectangular prism with the list inscribed on all four sides, found in 1992, like the other list it accounts for eight legendary rulers then simply proclaims that:

"Then the flood swept over. After the flood had swept over, and the kingship had descended from heaven, the kingship was in Kish …"

So here we have presumably legendary rulers going back far in time before the flood. This flood could possibly be the Great Flood of old, which the Bible spoke about and which many in the occult field like the Freemasons have said caused certain personages to hideaway secrets to be reinstated afterward. Albert Mackey, famous nineteenth-century author on Freemasonry, wrote about the preflood legends in his *The Legend of the Enoch*. Although not important to this work, it is a part of a long line of thinking in the esoteric field about the Great Flood and there being wisdom keepers like Enoch and Thoth who inscribed sacred sciences on stones prior to it to be found by us afterward. As is stated by Makey here:

"It is true that Enoch has been supposed to have been identical with Hermes, and ... Idris among the Hebrews, has been called Enoch, among the Egyptians Osiris and Hermes, and he was the first who before the Flood had any knowledge of astronomy and geometry ..."

This myth is deeply rooted within our human psyche or so it seems through these religious and quasi-religious writings. It is interesting to note that our oldest records attest to this and speak about legendary rulers going far back before it. This coupled again with the Kesh temple hymn would indicate that there is at least some history lost to us.

Famous eleventh-century Persian scholar and historian for the royal court of six different princes throughout his life, Abu Rayhan al-Biruni, wrote extensively on the ancient world. In addition to being a prolific mathematician, al-Biruni wrote an incredible academic work chronicling the history of the ancient world. This book, *Chronology of Ancient Nations,* spoke on the flood myth and more specifically the hidden preflood knowledge legend as well. In it al-Biruni states:

"It is related, that Tahmurath on receiving the warning of the Deluge—231 years before the Deluge—ordered his people to select a place of good air and soil in his realm … Thereupon, he ordered all scientific books to be preserved for posterity, and to be buried in a part of that place, least exposed to obnoxious influences …"

Tahumurath was a legendary rendition of Noah. Interestingly, writing in the early first millennium, al-Biruni was also probably one of the first to claim that the Great Flood left watermarks on the Pyramids of Giza, meaning they were built before the flood. This would be an extraordinary claim, depending on when you place the flood. Some would place it in a relatively recent ancient time while others would place it far into the prehistorical mythical times. Regardless it's an interesting claim and might show that our ancestors at the very least believed that these structures were older than that of the Egyptians.

This line of thinking was followed several years later by another scholar. Twentieth-century French philosopher, mystic, artist and scholar René Adolphe Schwaller de Lubicz wrote a mystical book titled *Sacred Science,* delving into various subjects involving Egyptian esotericism. In this book he too mentioned the Great Flood and claimed that there is geographical evidence of it on Egypt's monuments. Spending over a decade in the area in his early life, he was able to study the monuments up close in great detail. In his book he declared:

"A great civilization must have preceded the vast movements of water that passed over Egypt, which leads us to assume that the Sphinx already existed, sculptured in the rock of the west cliff at

Gizeh, that Sphinx whose leonine body, except for the head, shows indisputable signs of aquatic erosion."

Lubicz was under the impression that the erosion on the Giza Pyramids and Sphinx was due to heavy influxes of water, possibly the Great Flood of the Bible. This would place the Egyptian structures as being constructed much earlier in time, preceding mainstream history. As he speculated, they may have been constructed by an older, now lost civilization. It was Lubicz's work that would go on to inspire the more recent scholars to continue this theory. Famous alternative historian John Anthony West also furthered this discussion in his book *Serpent in the Sky*, published in 1979. With the help of his colleague, professor and geologist Robert Shoch, he concluded that Lubicz's observations may have been correct. If the Sphinx was weathered by heavy rains or flooding this could be evidence that it was built much earlier in history when the climate in that area would have produced such conditions. West places the date for the flooding as occurring about 15,000 BCE, when there were multiple glaciers melting around the world due to a sudden change in the earth's climate. West believed the implications of this theory to be of immense importance as we see in this quote from his book:

"If the single fact of the water erosion of the Sphinx could be confirmed, it would in itself overthrow all accepted chronologies of the history of civilisation; it would force a drastic reevaluation of the assumption of 'progress'—the assumption upon which the whole of modern education is based. It would be difficult to find a single, simple question with graver implications. The water erosion of the Sphinx is to history what the convertability of matter into energy is to physics."

In 1992 Robert Schoch was set to present his theory and debate it with other scholars at the annual meeting of the American Association for the Advancement of Science. The presentation didn't go as planned. Arguments broke out as the mainstream scholars scoffed and protested the information before the presentation could even start. Dr. Mark Lehner, representing the mainstream, is quoted as shouting, "I can't believe I'm involved in this debate, and that it is sanctioned by the AAAS," declaring that West's work was "pseudoscience." There is also evidence of heavy rains and flashfloods throughout ancient Egypt and even modern Egypt that could account for some of the erosion. Karl Lepsius (1810–1884) German Egyptologist, who is considered to be a founding father of Egyptology, wrote about a violent storm that suddenly erupted while he was undergoing some work at the Giza plateau. He is quoted as recounting the event in his book *Letters from Egypt, Ethiopia, and the Peninsula of Sinai* as follows:

"Suddenly the storm became a regular hurricane, such as I had never witnessed in Europe, and a hailstorm came down on us, which almost turned the day into night ... I suddenly saw a rapid mountain torrent precipitating, like a gigantic serpent on its certain prey, upon our encampment, already had it destroyed and beaten into the sand ... which united below the tents and was borne a hundred steps farther into a deep hollow behind the Sphinx, where a great lake, which fortunately had no outlet, formed itself in a moment."

Scholars on either side are in contention as to what has actually caused the erosion of the Sphinx. Some believe in the mainstream narrative of it being built during the third millennium BCE, while others believe it was built much earlier and possibly by a prehistory lost civilization.

Whether or not the Sphinx is older than its accepted date, we definitely have monuments that throw doubt into the accepted history of the human race. Until recent decades, it has been generally agreed that civilization stretches back only about 6-7000 years. In Turkey, not far from ancient Sumer we have the oldest known structure to date. Found by German archeologist Klaus Schmidt in 1994, Gobekli Tepe beautifully stands intact with enigmatic monuments going back to about 11-12,000 years BCE! Considered the oldest temple in the world, Ian Hodder, an anthropologist at Stanford University exclaims that:

"It's elaborate, it's complex, and it is pre-agricultural. That fact alone makes the site one of the most important archaeological finds in a very long time."

Having found no remnants of living quarters, cooking or trash, Schmidt and others concluded that the site was obviously used as some sort of sacred grounds. Sitting on top of a hill with a magnificent view, the site has various sections with upright stone slabs, similar to that of Stonehenge. There are no inscriptions found however there are carvings of animals, in particular that of vultures. There have also been human skulls found at the site with deliberate linear carvings embedded in them. Schmidt and others believe the site could have been a ceremonial or burial site for hunters. The symbol of the vulture could have held some meaning of death and

283

afterlife for the Gobekli Tepe builders. Of the site, Gary Rollefson, an archaeologist at Whitman College in Walla Walla, Washington pointed out: "There's more time between Gobekli Tepe and the Sumerian clay tablets than from Sumer to today,". Meaning there is a huge gap in time, making it hard to decipher cultural context of the site.

What's compelling about Gobekli Tepe is that it arose right around the time the last Ice age or the Pleistocene era ended which was about 11,700 years ago. We can imagine that age major glaciers of ice melted around the world, overtime certain areas were covered by new levels of water while others were revealed by the melting of ice. The change in climate allowed our ancestors to take hold of the land, to forage, domesticate and farm it. Some scholars such as Ian Hodder, as is pointed out in an article for Smithsonian Magazine titled, Gobekli Tepe: The World's First Temple, have concluded that in our ancient past humans first gathered to build religious structures and sites. Through this process we then progressed to building societies and cities, as opposed to the other way around. If Gobekli Tepe was erected shortly after the last Ice age this could mean that these people were possible witnesses to major cataclysms and the ending of the world they knew. The erecting of Gobekli Tepe could have been a way for them to ensure that some core beliefs of theirs were not lost, which could have been a paranoia of theirs having gone through the end of an era. It could have been a way to reinstate the core of their existence which centered around some religious belief lost to us now.

After all of this is considered I would conclude that whoever our progenitors were, be it the Anunnaki or whoever, they must have been humans from here. I don't doubt that this earth has been visited by peoples from other planets over its billions of years or that it has produced other species of humans with their own history, but the evidence simply isn't strong. The history isn't there. It's actually quite shocking how little we know about how we sprang up as a thinking and building species. In my mind there is no way our history simply starts about 5000 BCE with the onset of the Sumerians. As the legends attest there is a missing portion almost veiled behind an arrogant curtain of eroded and degraded records that if only pulled back, we could finally know the truth. It seems as if the evidence does point to some recently lost portion of our history due to some type of cataclysm be it the Great Flood, disease, war, or any other natural disaster. What is for certain is that the Anunnaki have been written by our ancestors to be those who pioneered earth and created us. This story was retold and added on to by many cultures that followed including the Old Testament. I believe if the Anunnaki were real at all they were humans, people who survived the cataclysm that severed us from prehistory and lived to speak about it. Not only did they live to speak about it, but they seized the opportunity to establish a hierarchy of rule where they and their family were seen as the royals whereas some of the younger, less intelligent were brought up to view themselves as the workers and servants of these divine people. Also, it is interesting that some of the earliest Sumerian tablets detail the Anunnaki as constructing the wild earth to be suitable and habitable for life. In one of the oldest known texts, *Enki and the World Order*, we see Enki being praised for a number of achievements. Among those, erecting shrines, and buildings, domesticating animals and helping other gods set up their establishments as well. As is recounted in these passages:

"He organised ploughs, yokes and teams. The great prince Enki bestowed the horned oxen that follow …, he opened up the holy furrows, and made the barley grow on the cultivated fields. Enki placed in charge of them the lord who wears the diadem, the ornament of the high plain, him of the implements, the farmer of Enlil … He made this good place perfect with grasses and herbs in abundance. He multiplied the animals of the high plain to an appropriate degree, he multiplied the ibex and wild goats of the pastures, and made them copulate …"

And as he's doing this, he bestows the responsibility to tend and watch over each station to another Anunna, thus organizing the newly found civilization of these royal people. Each praise is followed by Enki naming a respected and worthy Anunna to take charge of operating the area, which he builds and domesticates. For example, in this passage here he elects his father's friend to watch over a specific sheep and cow farm:

"He built the sheepfolds, carried out their cleaning, made the cow-pens, bestowed on them the best fat and cream, and brought luxury to the gods' dining places. He made the plain, created for grasses and herbs, achieve prosperity. Enki placed in charge of all this the king, the good provider of E-ana, the friend of An ..."

Enki is loved and remembered as the crafty and wise Anunna. He is praised as so in the text in this passage:

"I am the big brother of the gods, I bring prosperity to perfection. I am the seal-keeper of heaven and earth. I am the wisdom and understanding of all the foreign lands."

Continuing, as seen in this passage from Oxford's online translation, we see Enki being praised for creating the calendar system:

"Counting the days and putting the months in their houses, so as to complete the years and to submit the completed years to the assembly for a decision, taking decisions to regularise the days: father Enki, you are the king of the assembled people ..."

This text, which has precedent going all the way back to the early third millennium BCE, is subsequently detailing a time when society had to be organized, when agriculture and domestication had to be constructed. During this time there wasn't even a calendar to go by;

the Anunna were building from the ground up. What makes this text even more interesting is that the Anunnaki were not alone; they were not some isolated group of divine beings. The text mentions that Enki:

"Presented animals to those who have no city, to those who have no houses, to the Martu nomads …"

These people are briefly mentioned twice in the text as being nomads with no animals or houses. We're obviously not dealing with some quirky story about beings of creation forming the earth and magically creating life as we know it. This is a story about one group of people taking it upon themselves to upstart or maybe restart civilization. Nearby to them is another group who are less fortunate and have nothing to survive with, no home or food. With all of that I conclude that the Anunnaki as portrayed by our ancient ancestors were intelligent, smart, and savvy people who already knew how to organize a functioning infrastructure. They were survivors of a forgotten cataclysm or drastic change that might have killed off most of the inhabitants of the known world. These people, the Anunnaki, reinstated civilization and wrote themselves in the history of humanity as the gods.

Sources

[1] Mencken, H. L., Treatise on the Gods, Maryland Paperback Bookshelf, 1997, print.

[2] Ovason, David, The Secret Symbols of the Dollar Bill, 2004, Harper Collins, print.

[3] Levenda, Peter, The Secret Temple …, 2009, The Continuum International Publishing Group, print.

[4] Pike, Albert, Moral and Dogma …,1953, Edition Book Manufacturers, print.

[5] Norman, Jeremy, The Pyramid Texts: The Oldest Known Religious Texts, 12/21/21, https://www.historyofinformation.com/detail.php?entryid=2189.

[6] Dijk, J. v., Sasson, J. M. 1., & Baines, J. 1. (1995). Myth and Mythmaking in Ancient Egypt. *Civilizations of the Ancient Near East; 3, 3*, 1697–1709.

[7] Mark, Joshua J. "The Vedas." *World History Encyclopedia*. World History Encyclopedia, 9 Jun 2020. Web. 10 Jan 2022.

[8] "Rigveda." *New World Encyclopedia*, 28 Jul 2019, 15:55 UTC. 10 Jan 2022, 18:09 <https://www.newworldencyclopedia.org/p/index.php?title=Rigveda&oldid=1022482>.

[9 Badger, Richard G, Zoroastrianism and Judaism, The Gorham Press, 1918, print, Archive.org.

[10] "Avesta, as reproduced in the Divine Songs of Zarathushtra." World Religions Reference

Library. *Encyclopedia.com.* 29 Dec. 2021 <https://www.encyclopedia.com>.

[11] Mark, Joshua J. "Avesta." *World History Encyclopedia.* World History Encyclopedia, 8 Jan 2020. Web. 6 Jan 2022.

[12] Mark, Joshua J. "Zoroastrianism." *World History Encyclopedia.* World History Encyclopedia, 12 Dec 2019. Web. 6 Jan 2022.

[13] Brown, W. Norman. "The Creation Myth of the Rig Veda." *Journal of the American Oriental Society*, vol. 62, no. 2, American Oriental Society, 1942, pp. 85–98, https://doi.org/10.2307/594460.

[14] Ariel, David, How the Jews Invented God, and Made Him Great, June 5, 2018, Haaretz, https://www.haaretz.com/archaeology/.premium.MAGAZINE-how-the-jews-invented-god-and-made-him-great-1.5392677.

[15] Simonin, Antoine. "The Cyrus Cylinder." World History Encyclopedia. World History Encyclopedia, 18 Jan 2012. Web. 13 Jan 2022.

[16] Renger, Johannes M. "Hammurabi." Encyclopedia Britannica, 27 Mar. 2020, https://www.britannica.com/biography/Hammurabi. Accessed 25 March 2022.

[17] Carl Feagans, Sumerian Kings List and 241,000 Years of Rule, November 3, 2016, https://ahotcupofjoe.net/2016/11/sumerian-kings-list-and-241000-years-of-rule/.

[18] Spar, Ira. "Mesopotamian Creation Myths." In Heilbrunn Timeline of Art History. New York: The Metropolitan Museum of Art, 2000–.

http://www.metmuseum.org/toah/hd/epic/hd_epic.htm (April 2009).

[19] Fred Gladstone Bratton, Myths and Legends of the Near East, Thomas Y. Cromwell Company, 1970, print.

[20] Erika Marsal, A Brief History of Sumerology, June 2016, Friends of Asor, https://www.asor.org/anetoday/2016/06/brief-history-sumerology/.

[21] Sophie Hardach, The Key to Cracking the Long-Dead Languages?, 12/09/2018, Machine Minds, 12/09/2018 https://www.bbc.com/future/article/20181207-how-ai-could-help-us-with-ancient-languages-like-sumerian.

[22] Bipin Dimri, The Merovingians: Were these Dark Age Kings descended from Christ?, Historic Mysteries, https://www.historicmysteries.com/merovingian/.

[23] Alexander Stille, The World's Oldest Papyrus and What It Can Tell Us About the Great Pyramids, Oct. 2015, Smithsonian Magazine, https://www.smithsonianmag.com/history/ancient-egypt-shipping-mining-farming-economy-pyramids-180956619/, Web.

[24] Roger Pearse, The Log Book of Inspector Merer from Wadi al Jarf and the Pyramid of Cheops / Khufu, 09/27/17, https://www.roger-pearse.com/weblog/2017/09/27/the-log-book-of-inspector-merer-from-wadi-al-jarf-and-the-pyramid-of-cheops-khufu/comment-page-1/, Web.

[25] Seyfzadeh, M., & Schoch, R. M. (2018). The Inventory Stele: More Fact than Fiction. Archaeological Discovery, 6, 103–161. https://doi.org/10.4236/ad.2018.62007.

[26] Matthew Kirkham, Egypt Revelation: Great Pyramid of Giza's "correlation to Orion Proved," 01/21/2019, Express, https://www.express.co.uk/news/weird/1075135/egypt-great-pyramid-giza-orion-correlation-proof-spt.

[27] Ancient Code Team, The Great Pyramid of Giza is located at the exact center of The Earth's landmass, Unexplained, https://www.ancient-code.com/the-great-pyramid-of-giza-is-located-at-the-exact-center-of-earths-landmass/, Web.

[28] Tom Valentine, The Great Pyramid: Man's Monument to Man, 1975, Pinnacle Books, print.

[29] Jimmy Maher, How Alternative Egyptology and Scientific Archaeology Were Born on the Giza Plateau, 3/15/2020, Ars Technica, https://arstechnica.com/science/2020/03/how-alternative-egyptology-and-scientific-archaeology-were-born-on-the-giza-plateau/, Web.

[30] Frank Jacobs, St. Michael Alignment is England's Most Famous Ley Line. But is it Real?, 08/16/2011, Strange Maps, https://bigthink.com/strange-maps/527-the-st-michael-line-a-straight-story/, Web.

[31] A Chronology of European Geomancers, http://www.ancient-wisdom.com/leylines.htm, Web.

[32] Mark, Joshua J. "The Legend of Sargon of Akkad." World History Encyclopedia. World History Encyclopedia, 30 Aug 2014. Web. 14 Jun 2022.

[33] Vasile Ersek, How Climate Change Caused the World's First Ever Empire to Collapse, 1/03/2019, https://theconversation.com/how-climate-change-caused-the-worlds-first-ever-empire-to-collapse-109060.

[34] Dattatreya Mandal, The World's Oldest Known Pieces of Literature Pertain to Two Ancient Sumerian Works, July 21, 2016, https://www.realmofhistory.com/2016/07/21/world-oldest-known-literature-ancient-sumerian/.

[35] Mark, Joshua J. "Enheduanna." World History Encyclopedia. World History Encyclopedia, 24 Mar 2014. Web. 16 Jun 2022.

[36] Joseph R. Chambers, A Palace for the Antichrist, New Leaf Press, 1996, https://archive.org/details/palaceforantichr0000cham/page/n5/mode/2up?q=Saddam.

[37] Jack Van Ens, Why President Bush Blasts Babylon, Vail Daily, March 8, 2003, https://www.vaildaily.com/news/why-president-bush-blasts-babylon/.

[38] Ewan MacAskill, George Bush: "God Told Me to End the Tyranny in Iraq," World News, *The Guardian*, Fri 7 Oct 2005, https://www.theguardian.com/world/2005/oct/07/iraq.usa.

[39] James Doubek, An Ancient Tablet, Stolen Then Acquired By Hobby Lobby, Will Be Returned To Iraq, NPR, September 21, 2021, npr.org/2021/09/21/1039380004/gilgamesh-dream-tablet-hobby-lobby-iraq return#:~:text=Known%20as%20the%20Gilgamesh%20Dream%20Tablet%2C%20it%20was%20acquired%20by,and%20needed%20to%20be%20returned.

[40] Erin Brady, Million-Dollar "Gilgamesh Dream Tablet" Looted During Gulf War Finally Returned to Iraq, *Newsweek*, 12/07/21/, https://www.newsweek.com/million-dollar-gilgamesh-dream-tablet-looted-during-gulf-war-finally-returned-iraq-1657071.

[41] David R. Helm, 1–2 Peter and Jude: Sharing Christ's Sufferings, Crossway; Redesign edition, 2015.

[42] D. N. Campbell & Fika J. van Rensburg, A History of the Interpretation of 1 Peter 3:18–22, North West University, Acta Patristica et Byzantina, 2008, ResearchGate, April 22, 2019, https://www.researchgate.net/publication/26989896_History_of_the_interpretation_of_1_Peter_318-22?enrichId=rgreq-4add70a845aeb8aa2a4e6c8b5959b972-XXX&enrichSource=Y292ZXJQYWdlOzI2OTg5ODk2O0FTOjc1MDQwMDEwNTg5Nzk4NkAxNTU1OTIwNzM1NTc4&el=1_x_2&_esc=publicationCoverPdf.

[43] Goodspeed, Edgar J. "Some Greek Notes." *Journal of Biblical Literature*, vol. 73, no. 2, 1954, pp. 84–92. *JSTOR*, https://doi.org/10.2307/3261975. Accessed 10 Jul. 2022.

[44] The Book of Enoch, Translation by M. Knibb of the Ethiopian Text in the S.O.A.S. Library at the University of London.

[45] The Book of the Secrets of Enoch. Also known as Slavonic Enoch or 2 Enoch Translated from the Slavonic by W. R. Morfill, MA.

[46] Elizabeth Clare Prophet, Forbidden Mysteries of Enoch, Summit University Press, 1984, print.

[47] The Ante-Nicene Fathers, ed. Alexander Roberts and James Donaldson; 1885–1887; repr.
10 vols. (Peabody Mass: Hendrickson 1994).

[48] Hopler, Whitney. "Who Was the Angel Who Wrestled with Jacob?" Learn Religions, Feb. 8, 2021, learnreligions.com/angel-who-wrestled-with-jacob-124068.

[49] Benjamin R., Foster, From Distant Days: Myths, Tales, and Poetry of Ancient Mesopotamia, Bethesda, Md: CDL Press, 1995, print.

[50] TeSelle, Eugene (2002). *Augustine the Theologian*. Wipf and Stock. ISBN 978-1-57910-918-9.

[51] James Scott Trimm, Why the Rabbis Suppressed the Book of Enoch, 12.12.2019, Nazarene Space, http://nazarenespace.com/blog/2019/12/12/why-the-rabbis-suppressed-the-book-of-enoch/, Web.

[52] Jon D. Levenson, The Idea of Abrahamic Religions: A Qualified Dissent, 2010, Jewish Review of Books, https://tikvahfund.org/uncategorized/the-idea-of-abrahamic-religions-a-qualified-dissent/, Web.

[53] Vlaardingerbroek, H.M. / Mesopotamia in Greek and Biblical Perceptions: Idiosyncrasies and Distortions. 2014. p. 358.

[54] Aren M. Wilson-Wright, The Canaanite Languages, 2019, https://www.academia.edu/38629771/2019_The_Canaanite_Languages, Web.

[55] Jeremy M. Norman, The Mesha Stele, or Moabite Stone, a Non-Biblical Text, Confirms Some Events in the Biblical Book of Kings, 07/06/2022, https://www.historyofinformation.com/detail.php?id=5053.

[56] Paton, Lewis Bayles. "The Origin of Yahweh-Worship in Israel: II." The Biblical World, vol. 28, no. 2, 1906, pp. 113–27. JSTOR, http://www.jstor.org/stable/3141019. Accessed 1 Aug. 2022.

[57] Emerton, J. A. "'Yahweh and His Asherah': The Goddess or Her Symbol?" *Vetus Testamentum*, vol. 49, no. 3, 1999, pp. 315–37.

JSTOR, http://www.jstor.org/stable/1585374. Accessed 1 Aug. 2022.

[58] Paul D, The Origins of Yahweh and the Revived Kenite Hypothesis, 02/05/2016, https://isthatinthebible.wordpress.com/2016/02/05/the-origins-of-yahweh-and-the-revived-kenite-hypothesis/.

[59] Lawrence H. Schiffman, Ezra and Nehemiah
These two reformers charted a course for the future of Judaism., https://www.myjewishlearning.com/article/ezra-and-nehemiah/.

[60] Nadav Shragai, A Short History of Coexistence in Shimon HaTzadik, 04/20/2022, https://www.israelhayom.com/2022/04/20/a-short-history-of-coexistence-in-shimon-hatzadik/.

[61] Gianni Marchesi, The Sumerian King List or the "History" of Kingship in Early Mesopotamia, 11/2016, Friends of Asor, https://www.asor.org/anetoday/2016/11/sumerian-king-list-history-kingship-early-mesopotamia/.

[62] Raúl López, The Antediluvian Patriarchs and the Sumerian King List, 12/01/1998, Journal of Creation 12, no 3, https://answersingenesis.org/bible-history/the-antediluvian-patriarchs-and-the-sumerian-king-list/.

[63] De. C. Edward Sachau, The Chronology of Ancient Nations, 1879, London, Pub. for the Oriental translation fund of Great Britain & Ireland by W. H. Allen and co., Web, https://archive.org/details/chronologyofanci00biru/page/n3/mode/2up?q=deluge.

[64] Schwaller de Lubicz, R. A, Sacred Science: the King of Pharaonic Theocracy, New York: Inner Traditions International, 1982, Web,

https://archive.org/details/sacredsciencekin0000schw/mode/2up?q
=sphinx.

[65] Chris Ogilvie-Herald, Climate Change and the Age of the
Great Sphinx, 2020.

[66] David Bokovoy, Kar 4: An Example of Mesopotamian
Creation Motifs in Genesis, 12/10/2014, Web, When Gods Were
Men,
https://www.patheos.com/blogs/davidbokovoy/2014/12/kar-4-
an-example-of-mesopotamian-creation-motifs-in-genesis/.

[67] Saad D. Abulhab, Adam and the Early Mesopotamian
Creation Mythology, 2020, CUNY Academic Works.

[68] Mark Oliver, Inside The Mysteries Of Gobekli Tepe, The
Oldest Temple In The World, June 17, 2021,
https://allthatsinteresting.com/gobekli-tepe, web

[69] Andrew Curry, Gobekli Tepe: The World's First Temple?
Predating Stonehenge by 6,000 years, Turkey's stunning Gobekli
Tepe upends the conventional view of the rise of civilization,
Nov. 2008, Smithsonian Magazine,
https://www.smithsonianmag.com/history/gobekli-tepe-the-
worlds-first-temple-83613665/,web

Made in United States
Troutdale, OR
06/15/2023

10629155R00169